R0031 70016

Y0-AZH-167

CHICAGO PUBLIC LIBRARY
HAROLD WASHINGTON LIBRARY CENTER

R0031170016

LB 2832.2 .M87 Murphy, Judith.
Never too old to teach

Cop. 2

DATE			

THE CHICAGO PUBLIC LIBRARY

SOCIAL SCIENCES AND HISTORY DIVISION

© THE BAKER & TAYLOR CO.

NEVER TOO OLD TO TEACH

Never Too Old To Teach

by Judith Murphy
and Carol Florio

Academy for
Educational Development   AED

Academy for Educational Development, Inc.
680 Fifth Avenue
New York, New York 10019

Library of Congress Catalog Card Number: 78-50074
ISBN: 0-89492-001-4
Copyright © 1978 by Academy for Educational Development, Inc.
Printed in U.S.A.

CONTENTS

Introduction i

CHAPTER I:	Who Are These "Older People"?..	1
CHAPTER II:	The Nation's Need for Help in the Learning Process	13
CHAPTER III:	The Record to Date: A National View	19
CHAPTER IV:	A Record of Accomplishment: Some Cases in Point	39
CHAPTER V:	Guidelines for Program Development	63
CHAPTER VI:	Future Directions for Older Educators	75
CHAPTER VII:	Conclusions and Recommendations	83

APPENDICES

A. Survey Sample and Response	89
B. Statistical Tables from the 1976 AED Survey	91
C. A Sampling of Outstanding Educational Services Provided by Older Persons: Responses to the Survey	97
D. A Selected List of Local Programs and Projects in Which Older Persons Are Educating Others	103

As a young American concerned for the future of our nation, I am outraged and disgusted at the plight of our elderly. We treat our mothers, grandfathers, aunts, and uncles worse than we treat prisoners of war. The throw-away psychology we have developed since the Second World War permits us to forget about people once they reach 65. I can't think of a more unreasonable and unwise attitude for a nation to have.

Instead of cultivating our older citizens for their vitality, experience, wisdom, skills, maturity and intelligence, we shunt them off to one side. We turn our backs on them. We waste a national resource.

Sam Brown, Director of ACTION

Introduction

Demographers assure us that the "greying" of America is no passing phenomenon. For decades to come America may expect an increasing proportion of older citizens in the population. Today 22.9 million Americans (one in every ten) are 65 years of age or older; by the year 2030, 53 million people, or one in six, will be in this age group.

If Americans can refrain from construing the increase of the older population as one more threat to the existing order, one more intractable and costly problem, they can turn this development to everyone's advantage. This report contends that solving one "problem"—how to better the lot of older persons—can partially solve another problem—how to strengthen and enrich American education.

On one hand, as levels of education, health, and financial well-being rise within the older population, more and more of its members grow discontent with the passive-dependent role society has recently assigned to them, and seek new ways in which to lead full, useful lives.

One promising opportunity for older adults lies in educating roles. Millions of the men and women who now find themselves outside the job market have the vigor, background, and capacity to help people of all ages learn. Of these millions, as suggested by the study conducted for this report by the Academy for Educational Development, at least one million are now educating others throughout the vast reaches of our formal and informal education system. They teach, they counsel, they illuminate history with personal insights; they lead groups in self-awareness; they tutor everyone in everything. Most of them serve as volunteers, with a small fraction getting wages, stipends, or honoraria.

On the other hand, education in America stands in need of all the talented and imaginative help it can get. In the face of declining enrollments and rising costs, however, there is small likelihood that many older people will find or should be encouraged to look for renewed or second careers in conventional full-time teaching jobs.

The nation must find new ways to handle its educational resources, human and otherwise. Current cutbacks have exacerbated educational needs that were already severe. They are obvious throughout the whole spectrum of formal and informal education—from day care for preschool children to continuing education for adults, from the overcrowded classrooms of urban ghettoes to libraries, museums, settlement houses, and other community learning places. In school and out, in all these places and more besides, there is need for more people to help in the learning process.

We are rapidly becoming a nation of lifelong learners. As education refines its mission to include the needs of specialized groups of learners—from migrant children to professionals and managers—the scope of education grows constantly bigger and broader. In terms of demand, education is a strong growth industry. Seeking to develop educational means to meet these demands, education can logically look to the older population for assistance in reaching imaginative new solutions. The evidence suggests that such requests will find ready acceptance.

In general, society and the people who compose it benefit when there are chances for regular exchanges among the generations. Segregation by age shares the evils of any segregation. Interchange among the generations fosters a sense of the continuity of life, so lacking in urban, mobile 20th century America. It draws on different but complementary age-linked traits. In the words of 76-year-old Howard Rusk, head of the renowned New York University Institute of Rehabilitation Medicine, "It takes both old and young people to do a job. You need older people for stability and wisdom, and younger people for fire." Commingling of the generations benefits all: the young learn about work and life from a rich variety of older role models; for these older adults, the process acts as a powerful incentive to fulfill their highest potential.

Society best serves its members, whatever their age, when it allows them options—attractive and practical choices as to how they spend their lives, including its final decades. For millions of Americans, helping other people to learn represents a good choice.

This report describes a wide spectrum of programs that are successfully using older people in educating roles. As the Academy's survey showed, the older educators are successful, not only as evaluated by the sponsors of educational programs, but also in the eyes of their students, whether nursery school toddlers or graduate students or middle-aged adults or their own peers. Despite all this diversified activity, however, programs are still deficient in number and quality. And much needs to be done by way of evaluating and publicizing exemplary programs. Chapter 6 provides a set of general guidelines for the development of programs that can tap this "boundless resource," as Willard Wirtz has called America's older men and women.

Recruitment of older adults as educators is barely off the ground. Those at work today are nowhere near the number that society needs and could recruit. Like people of any age, older people do not ordinarily walk into a school, a library, a corporation, a museum, or any other place and offer their services. In most instances where older people are successfully filling educating roles, an institution or organization has sought them out.

It will take a concerted effort on the part of policy makers and administrators in government at all levels, in institutions, corporations, unions, organizations, and elsewhere, to fully realize the promise in the increased use of older people in teaching roles.

It is the policy makers who must instigate changes—in attitudes, guidance, training, compensation, and other incentives. Like the Academy's 1974 publication, *Never Too Old To Learn,* which dealt with study opportunities for older people, this report is aimed at those forces in society that are in a position to take appropriate steps. Though the subjects of this report may find it eye-opening, they are not the target audience. Rather than a barrage of cheery propaganda and uplift, older adults need to be presented with sensible and rewarding options. Then, there is every reason to believe, millions of older men and women will come forward to take their fitting roles in bringing American education much closer to what it could be.

This report, based upon evidence of what is now actually taking place, is an effort to bring the teaching activities of older Americans out of their obscurity, and to suggest ways in which these human resources may serve the learning needs of individuals and society at large.

ONE

Who Are These "Older People"?

Rather suddenly, it would appear, old age has become an "in" topic. Newsweeklies run cover stories on the "greying of America"; TV specials explore the condition and outlook of the aged; journals of opinion run sober analyses; major scandals break around nursing-home exploitation; scholars convene seminars; glamorous oldsters like Martha Graham and Eubie Blake and Ruth Gordon are feted; manufacturers, publishers, and other entrepreneurs cannily revise their marketing practices; universities add departments of gerontology; and retirees and pensioners themselves increasingly organize and fight for their rights. An aging America grows somewhat defensive about the nation's notorious apotheosis of youth. "Ageism" joins "childism" and "sexism" and "racism" to denote another prejudice for Americans to uproot.

How much good all this attention is doing for older Americans themselves is another question. Some good, undoubtedly, if only by highlighting issues and raising questions previously unasked. The flurry of notice brings dangers in its train, inevitably. One is its tendency to set the elders off as one more special-interest group, one more minority seeking redress of wrongs. While some such separatism may be essential if the aging are to achieve a more agreeable and fitting way of life, it risks the perils of divisiveness—entrapping its would-be beneficiaries still more tightly in the pigeonhole called age, and concurrently getting up the dander of younger Americans who may be led to see the old primarily as an ever-increasing threat to their own economic futures. One compelling difference, though, sets older people off from other victims of prejudice and misunderstanding. Unlike blacks, Jews, women, the impoverished, and the handicapped, the aged comprise a group that everybody may expect to belong to sooner or later.

Concentration on the aging *qua* aging runs the risk of reinforcing the stereotypes that hobble humane and imaginative solutions, of making still more hermetic what Wirtz has called life's "three time traps—education, then work, then obsolescence." The key to sound social policy on improving the lot of older people is to keep firmly in mind that "older people" are first of all people, individuals each in his own right.

With these warnings in mind, let us review some familiar statistics that provide a useful framework in which to consider these millions of individual men and women.

- More than one out of every ten Americans is 65 years of age or older.
- According to mid-1976 Census Bureau estimates, the 65-and-over population numbers about 22.9 million—an increase of 2.8 million since 1970—or 10.6 percent of the estimated total U.S. population of 215.1 million. Of the 22.9 million, nearly 60 percent are women.

- [ ] By the year 2030, if the present low birth rate and declining death rate hold steady, these older Americans will account for over 17 percent of the population, or one in every six Americans.
- [ ] Most men 65 and over are married and live with their wives. Only one out of seven is widowed; only one out of seven lives alone.
- [ ] By contrast, more than half the women in this age group are widowed, and more than a third of the women live alone. Only one-third are married and living with their husbands.
- [ ] Contrary to popular opinion, only a small proportion of the elderly population—about 5 percent in 1974—lives in institutions. (Over 80 percent of these are 75 and over.)
- [ ] Life expectancy for a boy born in 1973 is 67.6 years, for a girl 75.3 years, as against 46 years for a boy and 48 for a girl born in 1900. Most of these extra years of life expectancy have been achieved not through control of the process of aging but through improved sanitation and the conquest of the major fatal childhood diseases. A woman reaching 65 today can expect to live an additional 17.5 years; a man another 13.4 years.
- [ ] The annual income of older households averages $7,500. Because the typical household is now quite small, per capita income comes to $4,100, or 95 percent of the national norm. Twenty percent of older households have incomes in excess of $10,000. Yet some 3.4 million elderly persons, most of them single women, live in poverty, with annual household incomes of less than $3,500.
- [ ] Of all people 65 years old or more, about 3 million (or only 14 percent) were part of the work force in 1976. Of the total at work, close to 2 million were men, 1 million women. Since 1900

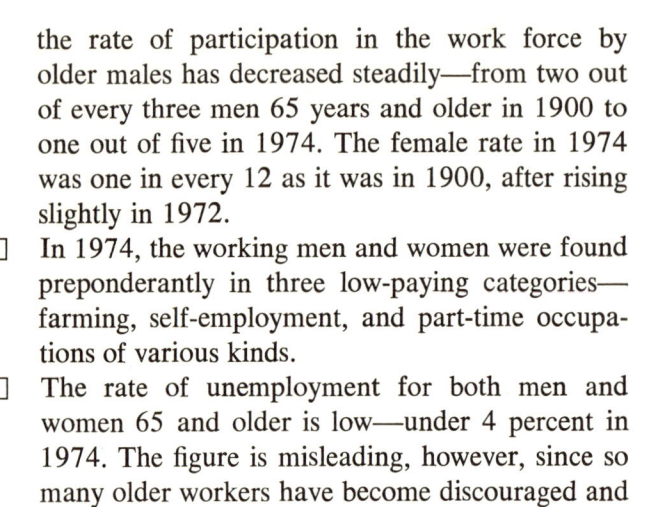

the rate of participation in the work force by older males has decreased steadily—from two out of every three men 65 years and older in 1900 to one out of five in 1974. The female rate in 1974 was one in every 12 as it was in 1900, after rising slightly in 1972.
- [ ] In 1974, the working men and women were found preponderantly in three low-paying categories—farming, self-employment, and part-time occupations of various kinds.
- [ ] The rate of unemployment for both men and women 65 and older is low—under 4 percent in 1974. The figure is misleading, however, since so many older workers have become discouraged and stopped looking for work, thus counting themselves statistically out of the labor market.
- [ ] As to formal education, the attainment of older people is still well below that of the overall adult population. In 1975, only about 35 percent of persons 65 and older were high school graduates, compared to about 62 percent of all adults 25 years old or more. But the level is rising for all adults, and by 1990 about half the people 65 and over are expected to be high school graduates. (As recently as 1952 it was only 18 percent.)

This basic statistical profile of Americans aged 65 and over indicates that, *on the average,* they are not working or looking for work; that they include substantially more women than men, and that the women are much more apt to be widowed and living alone. Only a minority finished high school. The picture thus far is primarily derived from census returns, and is necessarily painted in broad strokes.

For more revealing detail about the 65-and-over population, it is necessary to look elsewhere. Thanks to the work of physicians, psychologists, and a variety of scholars, it is possible to understand much better than before what aging means and what it does *not* mean. This understanding has been further enhanced by that quintessentially modern tool, the scientific survey, notably the 1974 poll completed by Louis Harris and Associates for the National Council on the Aging. It is the most extensive study of attitudes on aging ever conducted in the United States.

The Harris study is aptly called *The Myth and Reality of Aging in America.* Myths about old age are persistent and hard to eradicate; they persist among all age groups including the aged themselves who, after all, were but lately young themselves. Thus, a person 65 or older tends to consider himself the exception and, along with the rest of the population, to lump all *other* older people together as not terribly bright or alert, adaptable or resilient or open-minded, although usually warm and friendly and wise from experience. Studies made in the 1960's and 1970's suggest that society's view of the aged has its roots in childhood. In 1976 a University of Maryland study of children's attitudes toward the elderly produced responses like "sick, sad, tired, dirty and ugly, wrinkled, crippled, chew funny and haven't any teeth." The same children, however, tended to view old people as "friendly, good, kind, rich, and wonderful."

One of the most persistent myths, very slowly losing its grip, is the notion that senility is somehow inevitably linked with aging, and that mental and temperamental vigor and capacity are bound to decline with physical vigor. We know now that there is no such correlation. A minority of old people do become senile for reasons still unknown. The unhappy denouement may be the product of particular genetic and/or experiential causes, perhaps even diet. It is not the automatic outcome of years lived. Alex Comfort, author of *The Joy of Sex* and a leading gerontologist, is not one to mince words. "Crazy" is his word for "senile," and he has written: "Old people become crazy for three reasons: because they were crazy when young, because they have an illness, or because we drive them crazy," and he points out that "rather fewer old people are crazy than at earlier ages."

According to Dr. Daniel T. Peak, a psychiatrist at Duke University's Center for Aging, successful aging most often follows successful youth and middle years. But even without this felicitous prologue, a person is not condemned to an unsatisfactory old age. Stressing for the later years what commentators from Erickson on down to Sheehy have been saying about the whole of life, Dr. Peak discounts the "social delusion" that "growth and development stop when one reaches early adulthood." Change is possible at almost any age. It depends on the individual. "Old people," as Jack Ossofsky, director of the National Council on the Aging, recently told *The St. Petersburg Times,* "are usually what they were when they were younger, only more so. What we need to do is to begin separating out those older people with problems instead of thinking of older people's problems."

Overall, certain mental capacities do tend to diminish with age—for instance, the capacity to immediately recall new facts or events as well as one remembers the more distant past. In part, however, even this failing is mythically induced, in young and old alike. Samuel Johnson makes the point: "There is a wicked inclination in most people to suppose an old man decayed in his intellect. If a young or middle-aged man, when leaving a company, does not recollect where he laid his hat, it is nothing; but if the same inattention is discovered in an old man, people will shrug up their shoulders and say, 'His memory is going.' " And, of course, the old man is inclined to agree and help perpetuate the myth.

In combatting the myths and fears and prejudices that becloud old age, however, it is essential to avoid the opposite danger of idealizing and thus equally falsifying this time of life. We might do well to eschew Browning and his "best is yet to be, the last of life for which the first was made," in favor of Maurice Chevalier and his common-sensical view:

"Am I looking forward to old age? Yes, considering the alternative!".

Frank Reissman, editor of the bimonthly *Social Policy,* in his introduction to a 1976 issue devoted to "older persons," struck a good balance on this particular question:

> ... In their genuine efforts to eliminate negative stereotypes, too many "gerontophiles" have tended to deny the real difficulties associated with aging. My own personal experience of aging has shown me that reflexes slow down, mental functioning is at least different, a subtly more conservative outlook emerges, and death becomes a more important concern.
>
> Although I have an extremely active intellectual and athletic life as well as a fulfilling family life, I do experience aging in my bones, in my mind, in my emotions, and my attitudes. It takes me longer to recover from illnesses, my reflexes on the tennis court are not as sharp, maintaining a desirable weight is hard, learning new games and new ideas is not as easy.

Again, this is the view of one man, obviously a member of the "young-old" generation, who is well-off, active, and variously blessed. The Reissman statement illustrates once more how critical it is to bear in mind that "older people" or "senior citizens" or "the aging" are *not* a bloc, not a monolith, not a census abstraction. Like blacks, or Hispanics, or youth, they have only certain things in common. As a group what they chiefly share, besides age, are the by-products of the aging process, and—extrinsically—the assets and debits of society's arrangements for the 65-and-over population. Carolyn Setlow, of Louis Harris and Associates, makes the point lucidly:

> Above all else, the 65 and over group have lived longer than the rest of the public. More than any other factor, older people share with each other their chronological age. Yet the research shows that factors more powerful than age alone determine the conditions of one's later years. Instead, the aspirations and disappointments, the life satisfactions and dissatisfactions, the personalities and problems that defined them as individuals when they were younger continue to make them unique in their later years.
>
> In short, there appears to be no such thing as the typical experience of old age nor the typical older person. At no point in one's life does a person stop being himself and suddenly turn into an "old person," with all the myths and stereotypes that that term involves.

The fallacy of overgeneralizing about the elderly is clear from the statistics already cited, whether the specific is health or education or marital status or income or living arrangements. On any given aspect of later life, one can often say "many" persons but seldom "most" and never "all" or "almost all." This diversity also prevails in the picture derived from statistics of the older American's attitudes toward work and retirement. As figures cited earlier showed, only a small fraction (14 percent) of people 65 and older were still part of the work force in 1976.

The Harris poll discovered, in questioning retired or unemployed older people, that the majority expressed no interest in returning to work. But the minority expressing a desire to work was sizable—nearly 7 million people, or better than three out of ten. Least happy with unemployment were the members of the lowest income group.

Poor health was the major reason cited for not working despite the expressed desire to do so. More than twice as many people (57 percent) named this obstacle as did the next most cited obstacle (the 28 percent who simply said "too old"). The Harris study, however, reached the interesting conclusion that the preeminence of "poor health" among reasons for not working may well be "a learned excuse to cover up for other reasons such as 'nobody wants me,'" a more acceptable and less embarrassing justification for not working. The study went on to suggest another interpretation of health problems among the aging: "a causal relationship between enforced idleness and health." According to a 1972 study by the American Medical Association:

> There is ample clinical evidence that physical and emotional problems can be precipitated or exacerbated by denial of employment opportunities. Few physicians deny that a direct relationship exists between enforced idleness and poor health. The practitioner with a patient load comprised largely of older persons is convinced that the physical and emotional ailments of many . . . are a result of inactivity imposed by denial of work.

The Harris survey probed some of the social and economic facts of life behind older people's assertion of being "too old" to work, making it apparent that often this was less a self-diagnosis than a reflection of prevailing attitudes and mores and, to some extent, law. Most pension policies set age 65 for mandatory retirement. Even more influential in making 65 synonymous with the onset of old age was the quite arbitrary decision, in 1935, to gear full retirement benefits to that age in the new Social Security system. Moreover, even the Age Discrimination in Employment Act of 1967 protects persons only up the age of 65, not beyond. So no matter how well a man or woman of 64 realizes that the next birthday is not going to change him from middle-aged to elderly overnight, it is difficult to buck the combined weight of all these social forces.

Discrimination among employers against older people is widespread and incontrovertible. The barriers, in fact, loom larger than those facing any other age group, and this despite well-documented evidence that older people perform well on the job, and that most of the public believes they do.

What the ground-breaking Harris survey showed about older people and work was, in sum, that the population of persons 65 and over who want to work extends far beyond the 14 percent now gainfully employed (most of them part time) and beyond the more than 20 percent engaged in volunteer work. These millions of men and women constitute an important source of manpower. Many of them feel that they have particular skills or capacities that they would like to use given the chance. Nearly 3 million people expressed an interest in learning new skills, taking part in job-training programs, and embarking on new or renewed careers; the figure would doubtless be higher were it not for the well-known barriers to the employment of older people.

There remains, in this review, the matter of volunteer work—which some people, young and old, regard as distinct from *real* work, and which prompts controversy within union circles, the women's movement, and elsewhere. According to the Harris poll, over 20 percent of the public 65 and older report doing volunteer work; the percentage is considerably higher among the better off and better educated. The kinds of work are not much different than volunteer work done by the population generally—a great variety of jobs in fields one might expect: health, civic affairs, social services (e.g., hot-line counseling, visiting the homebound), give-away programs (e.g., thrift shops, distribution of food in emergencies), and service geared to families and children (e.g., day care, teaching home management skills). Health and mental health came out on top of all the categories, claiming 23 percent of the older volunteers. In seeking to pinpoint the jobs for which older people volunteer, the Harris survey devised a dozen and a half categories. Since many respondents checked off their participation in more than one category, there is no neat statistical way to rank the fields quantitatively.

It is at first surprising to find "education" way down the line in the survey replies, with only 9 percent of the volunteers so engaged. Upon further examination, however, the table reveals that perhaps as many as 20 percent of all older volunteers are involved in work that is broadly educational. For the survey designers limited "education" strictly to such school-related roles as teacher aides, tutors, and storytellers. To the 9 percent involved in such activities it seems fair to add at least another 11 percent of all responding volunteers. Many of those in the health field surely are teaching, or "educating," in their work with family planning, drug abuse, alcoholism, programs for the mentally disturbed. And many, if not most of the respondents in seven or eight other categories are contributing their time in capacities that are properly, if not officially, those of teachers or trainers. Included here, for example, would be most of those engaged in "cultural activities" (e.g., teaching art, theatre for young people, general enrichment opportunities, museum tours, sponsoring art centers), some of those working in "nutrition" (which includes teaching food selection and preparation), and most of the volunteers working on the "physical environment," (which covers conservation drives, playground and park development, and the like).

In the real numbers, the present volunteer force among older people is 4.5 million. According to the Harris study, however, the figure understates the potential. Another 10 percent of the public aged 65 and over and not now engaged in volunteer work say they would like to be, thus suggesting a volunteer force (actual and potential) of nearly 7 million older Americans.

Not every or almost every older American would, given the chance, opt for working, at a "real" job or as a volunteer. Many are beset by poor health, lack of mobility, and assorted cares; some of them really are "too old." Others, after a lifetime of drudgery or unrewarding work, are disposed now that they can to take life easy. Still others are happily endowed with absorbing friends, family, avocations, and interests. Not everybody subscribes to the bad press that retirement now gets. Nor are all the elderly as down on leisure and as gung ho for work as some of their more doctrinaire apologists seem to assume. A cautionary analogy could be drawn to an early and malign byproduct of the women's movement, whereby reasonably contented wives and mothers were made to feel uneasy or even guilty for not entering or wanting to enter the work force.

Nonetheless, an increasing number of men and women who have retired, or are about to retire, and who no longer bear heavy family responsibilities want to play active roles in life for as long as possible, whether in paying or unpaid jobs. They are not resigned to an endless vista of knitting, model-building, bingo, TV, or competitive valetudinarianism. It is clear that an indeterminate, but large, number of these older Americans are equipped and willing to make life better for themselves and others through a great diversity of *educational* roles.

Is this an elite minority of the robust, well-off, well educated? Probably most of these men and women belong to the "happy few." But by no means all of them. For, as succeeding chapters will demonstrate, many of society's educational needs can be filled by people whose prime qualification is not credentialed expertise but experience, warmth, and judgment. As it happens, these rank high among the positive qualities attributed to older people by the general public. And sometimes they are easiest found in men and women who belong to the minorities created by race and poverty.

TWO

The Nation's Need for Help In the Learning Process

In his influential and unexpectedly popular book, *Small Is Beautiful,* E. F. Schumacher has a chapter called "The Greatest Resource—Education." It begins by describing the unprecedented energy that Western civilization has devoted to organized education, and our apparent conviction of education's power as "the key to everything." It would appear that much good can come of devising imaginative ways to match one "boundless resource"—older people—with the needs of that "greatest resource"—education.

American education needs all the help it can get, *for* every category of learner, whether toddlers or elders, as it needs help *from* everybody who can facilitate the learning process. In this sense, to borrow John Holt's formulation in his book, *Freedom and Beyond,* society needs teachers (with a small "t") as well as credentialed Teachers.

Controversies swirl, as ever, around the how and what of education. With the back-to-basics crowd one must agree that many if not most of the young people today are far from achieving true literacy; with the radical school reformers, that education has failed to exploit the resources of the communities that lie outside school walls; with the career-education evangelists, that we have yet to devise practical and fulfilling ways to prepare students for the workplace, much less for life.

One way to meet some of education's current needs is to tap the relatively untapped resource represented by men and women aged 65 and older.

"Age doesn't mean automatic wisdom, of course," as gerontologist James Birren told an interviewer in 1976. "It only means more experiences." But for many older people these experiences add up to the maturity that can cope with life—and "that's wisdom," said Dr. Birren.

Where and how could this reserve of functional (if not credentialed) teachers help to enhance learning in the United States? First, in the schools themselves, where unresolved problems aggravated by inflation have eliminated teachers, increased class size, reduced the ranks of "paraprofessionals," and once again diluted the schools' ever-meager "cultural enrichments," those offerings in the arts and humanities that some would deem all-important but which always fall as expendable "frills" to budget-slashers.

Communities large and small all over the country are unable to provide enough capable teachers or mentors or guides for everyone who needs or wants to learn. As a result students or would-be students are being short-changed. There is no intention here of raising the tired old argument about class size; dogged studies by educationists down the decades have failed to establish, one way or the other, a correlation between class size and individual achievement. Let us simply accept the testimony of experience and common sense that one teacher with a class of 48 second-graders will have a rougher time turning them into competent readers than will a teacher responsible for 20 or 30 children who may have access as well to specialists and classroom helpers.

Learning to read may stand here for the whole range of basic tools that a person needs to make his way in today's world. Evidence abounds, from anecdotes current in almost any social circle to elaborate statistics, of how much wise and interested one-to-one intervention counts in overcoming individual reading problems or in preventing them. Indeed, a recent report by the National Assessment of Educational Progress, headlined in *The New York Times* as "Reading Skills Are Making a Comeback," attributes the gain in the reading ability of nine-year-olds to the flow of government funds into primary education over the decade from 1965 to 1975, which meant the use of reading specialists to work with small groups of children and of paraprofessional teacher aides.

Little such help has been afforded to secondary school students, in whose reading ability the National Assessment reports no reversal of recent downhill trends. (And the deficit compounds as students with minimal ability to read or write go on to colleges, which try to provide belated help.)

Another area of great and growing deprivation is day care. All over the United States, state and city budget slashes have curtailed the funding of day care centers, forcing many to close, preventing others from making essential improvements. This attrition comes at a time when more mothers than ever before are working outside the home. Early in 1977 the Labor Department reported that 46 percent of American children under eighteen had mothers with outside jobs, compared to 39 percent in 1970. An estimated 30 percent of these women are mothers of preschoolers.

Only a small fraction of the mothers with preschool children are working so that they can buy luxuries. Another small fraction command paychecks large enough to pay the high cost of good private day care. The great majority of these mothers are supporting or helping to support their families, and cannot afford private day care; 20 percent are heads of one-parent families. The lack of adequate provision for day care not only penalizes millions of mothers and creates a barrier to education, training, and jobs, it also means that much of the day care that is available amounts to little more than institutional baby-sitting. Under present budget constraints, therefore, poor programs and too few caring, imaginative, and experienced adults are getting members of the youngest generation off to a shaky start.

If such gaps exist in what might be called the bread-and-butter of education—institutions for the young from preschool through college—it is hardly surprising to find similar or worse gaps in educational enterprises outside these formal bounds. One is in the vast amorphous and expanding field of adult—or "continuing" or "lifelong"—education, whose clients range from unemployed high school dropouts to the very old. Just as varied as the clientele is the educational substance, which includes everything from car repair and learning English as a second language to high-level course work in linguistics or engineering. Groups with different kinds of educational needs include:

- ☐ Functionally illiterate adults, who need instruction in basic skills, health, nutrition, legal matters, consumer affairs, political participation
- ☐ The retarded, the handicapped, the incapacitated old, the imprisoned and otherwise institution-bound, who need gifted and highly individual instruction
- ☐ Adults of all ages who want to expand their knowledge and understanding in any one of countless fields, for their own pleasure and enlightenment or for vocational reasons
- ☐ The unemployed or underemployed who need solid up-to-date training in order to get jobs or better jobs

Many sources of education lying outside the so-called

educational system are a part of the real educational process, some of them by tradition and explicit intent, others implicitly or potentially. Aside from the vast educational enterprise run by industry, they are mostly public or quasi-public. And nearly all of them (again with the exception of corporations) have suffered the same attrition and staff-cutting that afflicts the public services in general at a time when demand is on the ascendant. For example:

- ☐ *Public libraries.* Historically serving as free and open universities to inquiring students young and old, many libraries have been forced to cut staff, diminish services, and shorten hours.
- ☐ *Museums of art, science, technology, history.* Their predicament is like that of the libraries, as is their educating function. Museums notably have long depended on volunteers, including the middle-aged to elderly, for much of their "education" function. As this function grows more important, there are some promising portents of the better use of volunteers.
- ☐ *Hospitals, clinics, health centers.* Spiraling costs and customers and the controversies about health care reflect critical conditions everywhere. Paramedical help is needed for a great variety of duties, particularly in the areas of preventive health education and counseling, home care and rehabilitation.
- ☐ *Extension Service of the U.S. Department of Agriculture.* This giant educational arm of the government is now being pressed, at a time when austerity rules budgets at all levels, to meet an unprecedented array of demands, from consumer guidance to environmental education to the improvement of all aspects of rural life.
- ☐ *Senior centers.* As more and more of these are established around the country, demands to im-

prove and expand their programs have arisen. A particular unfilled need—as is true for low-income adults generally—is for sound education on consumer affairs and political action.

Other less obvious but important places of learning that need more able and willing hands to help in their work include local governments, parks and recreation programs, organized efforts to conserve the natural and the man-made environment and to preserve cultural history, public interest groups in many fields, corporate programs for training or upgrading workers, churches deeply rooted in community service, and an enormous diversity of community-based art groups.

Short of structural changes in American society, there is little reason to expect increased public or private outlays for education. As in all sectors of life, the time has come for conservation, for imaginative and novel making-do with what we have, for finding what the New York Urban Coalition, talking specifically about classroom problems, recently called "affordable solutions."

"All history," says E. F. Schumacher, "as well as all current experience points to the fact that it is man, not nature, who provides the primary resource: that the key factor of all economic development comes out of the mind of man." One specific primary resource available now but severely underused is America's older men and women. There is ample evidence that a great many of these people are not only bringing to teaching the warm-hearted individual attention most students need if they are to learn, but are also conveying a sense of the *ends* of education, and of the rewarding satisfactions that grow out of learning how to read and write or of acquiring knowledge of any kind.

THREE

The Record to Date: A National View

To assert that older adults can help solve exigent educational problems is a compelling proposition. To establish its validity, however, and to spur further progress requires the backing of fact. How many older persons are actually filling educational roles? What precisely are they doing? How well are they doing it? What programs encourage their participation? Does the record offer insight into the variety of people at work, and into the variety of educational work they do?

In 1976, the Academy for Educational Development sent questionnaires to 11,500 schools, colleges, and other nonprofit organizations with strong educational missions to find out the extent to which they were using the services of people aged 65 and over in educating roles; to identify the types of roles older people were playing; and to determine how satisfactory the host institutions found the performance of their older workers.

THE SURVEY FINDINGS

Among the nation's formal and nonformal educational institutions:

- ☐ The use of older people in educating roles is the rule rather than the exception, but the number of older persons per institution or school district is typically low.
- ☐ The deployment of older adults varies markedly from one type of institution to another.
- ☐ Older persons perform well in a wide spectrum of educational roles.

During the late summer of 1976 questionnaires were mailed to all public school districts serving 5,000 or more students, one half of the colleges and universities in the United States, the Institutes of Lifetime Learning sponsored by the American Association of Retired Persons, all museums with designated education directors, and all of the following: senior centers and clubs offering educational programs, public libraries, Jewish community centers and YM-YWHAs, YWCAs, YMCAs, and 4-H clubs. Appendix A provides a detailed description of the survey sample and response.

The following pages present the findings of this survey, based on the experiences of 3,145 responding institutions in 1975-76.

Three out of four institutions had used the services of older adults in "educating" roles. Table A illustrates that this percentage varied little among types of institutions.

TABLE A

Percentage of Institutions Using the Services of Older Adults in Education-related Roles, 1975-76

Type of Institution	Percent
ALL INSTITUTIONS	77.1
Public school districts	74.2
Two-year colleges	75.0
Senior colleges and universities	78.8
Institutes of Lifetime Learning	100.0*
Museums	77.1
Senior centers and clubs	92.5*
Public libraries	59.0
Jewish community centers & YM-YWHAs	73.3
YWCAs	79.0
YMCAs	47.2
4-H clubs	87.8

*Both Institute of Lifetime Learning and senior center educational programs are run by as well as for senior adults.

Source: Academy for Educational Development, 1976

Although the percentage of institutions using the services of older adults is consistently high, the number of older persons serving at individual institutions is quite low. Findings indicate that the *average* number of older adults in educating roles ranges from a high of 33 at senior centers and Institutes of Lifetime Learning to a low of seven at public libraries. (See Table 1 in Appendix B.)

Educating Roles

While older adults are serving in a wide range of educating roles, fifteen roles appear to be most significant, in terms both of the number of institutions reporting such workers, and of the number of these older workers. They are:

>Activity or project leader
>Resource person or special lecturer
>Teacher
>Tutor
>Group leader
>Educational advisory committee member
>Teaching aide
>Library aide or librarian
>Curriculum consultant
>Counselor
>Administrator of education program
>Media production staff member
>Creator of educational games and classroom aids
>Researcher
>Tour guide or docent

Two thirds of all older people working in educational roles do so as activity or project leaders, resource persons or special lecturers, teachers, and tutors. The first three roles account for over one half of all older workers. (Table 2 in Appendix B lists the fifteen most common roles in rank order according to the number of older persons performing them in the responding institutions.)

The survey also revealed that:

- ☐ Fourteen percent of all older persons in the schools and 10 percent of those in two-year colleges are teaching aides.
- ☐ At least 10 percent of all older persons in the Institutes of Lifetime Learning and in all of the Ys serve as members of educational advisory committees.

- ☐ Not unexpectedly, 27 percent of the older adults working in public libraries are library aides (or sometimes librarians).
- ☐ In both two-year and senior colleges 7 percent of the older adults are curriculum consultants.
- ☐ Ten percent of the older persons serving in the senior colleges hold administrative positions.
- ☐ Twelve percent of the older adults working in the public libraries are involved in media production.
- ☐ In the museums, 27 percent of all older persons are serving as docents, another 10 percent as researchers.

(Table 3 in Appendix B gives the percentages of older people in 15 major educating roles in the types of institutions surveyed.)

Other positions for older people identified by the survey include "foster grandparents" (who work with mentally retarded children), coaches, media technicians, interpreters, placement counselors, board members and trustees, museum curators and assistants, houseparents, bookstore managers, fund raisers, alumni liaison officers, camp and recreation aides, and speech therapists.

Patterns of Deployment

Conglomerate statistics blur important differences in the way various types of institutions use older adults. (See Table 4 in Appendix B.)

To illustrate deployment differences it may be helpful to imagine how a theoretical institution of each type is likely to assign its average-sized staff of older adults.

The theoretical job rosters on the following pages are based on data from Tables 1, 3, and 4 in Appendix B. In each case it can be assumed that the last jobs on the roster would be the last to be filled.

How a Typical Institution Might Assign an Average Number of Older Adults to Educating Roles

A SCHOOL DISTRICT:
average 35 older adults

13 tutors
8 resource people
5 teaching aides
3 teachers
3 library aides
1 creator of educational games
1 administrator
1 curriculum consultant

A 4-H CLUB:
average 21 older adults

10 activity leaders
3 group leaders
2 teachers
2 resource people
1 educational advisory committee member
1 counselor
1 curriculum consultant
1 administrator or media production person

A TWO-YEAR COLLEGE:
average 12 older adults

4 teachers
3 resource people
1 teaching aide
1 curriculum consultant
1 person in "another" educating role
1 administrator
1 library aide or librarian

A SENIOR COLLEGE OR UNIVERSITY:
average 8 older adults

3 teachers
1 resource person
1 administrator
1 library aide or librarian
1 curriculum consultant
1 tutor

AN INSTITUTE OF LIFETIME LEARNING:
average 33 older adults

14 group leaders
6 teachers
3 educational advisory committee members
2 resource people
2 people in "another" educating role
1 activity leader
1 curriculum consultant
1 administrator
1 counselor
1 media production person
1 tutor or researcher

A SENIOR CENTER:
average 33 older adults

8 activity leaders
7 resource people
6 teachers
5 group leaders
2 educational advisory committee members
1 tutor
1 media production person
1 counselor
1 administrator
1 curriculum consultant or researcher

A PUBLIC LIBRARY:
average 7 older adults

2 library aides
1 resource person
1 media production person
1 person in "another" educating role, i.e. outreach
1 activity leader
1 tour guide or teacher

A YWCA:
average 15 older adults

4 activity leaders
3 teachers
2 resource people
2 group leaders
1 educational advisory committee member
1 tutor
1 counselor
1 curriculum consultant

A YM-YWHA or JEWISH COMMUNITY CENTER:
average 33 older adults

7 activity leaders
7 teachers
6 resource people
4 group leaders
4 educational advisory committee members
1 tutor
1 curriculum consultant
1 library aide
1 counselor
1 administrator

A MUSEUM:
average 16 older adults

4 docents
3 resource people
2 activity leaders
1 teacher
1 researcher
1 library aide
1 media production person
1 group leader
1 person in "another" educating role, i.e. outreach
1 educational advisory committee member

A YMCA:
average 9 older adults

2 activity leaders
1 resource person
1 teacher
1 group leader
1 educational advisory committee member
1 counselor
1 media production person
1 person in "another" educating role, i.e. camp or recreation aide

For Love or Money

The vast majority of older adults (over 90 percent) who serve in educating roles are volunteers. Four percent of these volunteers receive a stipend to cover expenses. Ten percent are paid employees. With so mixed a sample population, however, there are significant deviations from this "average" pattern, as shown in Table B below.

In higher education, for example, older people are almost evenly divided between paid employees and volunteers, with nearly 20 percent of the volunteers receiving stipends. Paid employees 65 and over in the public schools and other organizations, however, are very much the exception. A full 88 percent of older adults serving the schools do so as unpaid volunteers. (This contrast was predictable, in the light of higher education's generally less stringent and uniform regulations governing retirement.) In the nonschool organizations, the proportion of volunteers ranges from two-thirds to virtually all.

TABLE B

Employment Status of Older Adults in Educating Roles at 2,426 Institutions

Type of Institution	Unpaid Volunteers	Stipended Volunteers	Paid Employees
Public school districts	88	2	10
Two-year colleges	53	12	35
Senior colleges and universities	27	7	66
Institutes of Lifetime Learning	41	46	13
Museums	90	1	9
Senior centers and clubs	87	6	7
Public libraries	79	6	15
Jewish community centers & YM-YWHAs	86	2	12
YWCAs	66	26	8
YMCAs	88	3	9
4-H clubs	99	1	0
ALL INSTITUTIONS	86%	4%	10%

Source: Academy for Educational Development, 1976

Performance Rating

A highlight of the survey findings is the impressive rating that all institutions gave to the performance of their older workers. On a five point scale—with five points representing excellent and one representing poor—85 percent of the institutions rated their older workers as excellent or very good. The breakdown was as follows:

Excellent	43.6%
Very good	42.2
Average	8.1
Below average	0.5
Poor	0.0
No response	5.6
TOTAL	100.0%

Coordination with Outside Programs

About one fifth of all institutions using older adults in educating roles reported that some (generally less than 25 percent) of them came through cooperative arrangements with outside volunteer programs. Nineteen percent reported cooperation with a Retired Senior Volunteer Program (RSVP), 22 percent with a local, state, or regional volunteer program. This finding confirms the prevalent notion that most of the older people serving in educational settings are there because they have been recruited by the institutions they serve.

Table 5 in Appendix B illustrates the degree of coordination with outside volunteer programs among the different types of institutions surveyed.

The survey also sustained the validity of another common assumption: that many older people engaged in educational roles fill their jobs, not as the outcome of any deliberate campaign on the part of the institution, but rather as a by-product of tradition or overall policy. Many colleges and universities, for instance, employ a fair number of older faculty and administrators simply because tradition has set the maximum retirement age at age 70, rather than the mandatory 65 that usually applies in the lower schools. Furthermore, such community institutions as museums and libraries have long depended on the availability of older volunteers, primarily women. Occasionally, however, universities and other educational institutions have undertaken programs specifically devised to take advantage of the educational talents of older men and women.

"Outstanding and/or unique..."

The survey yielded a wealth of specifics in response to a query about "older individuals who provided outstanding and/or unique services." In some instances, responding institutions demurred from singling out individuals ("Impossible to identify a few," "All were unique and outstanding in their own way"), or from naming names.

Throughout the replies ran a stream of praise for the qualities manifested by older workers: dedication, enthusiasm, reliability, industry, creativity, resourcefulness, energy, patience, efficiency, skill, knowledge, cooperativeness, serenity. Appendix C provides the merest sampling from the hundreds of outstanding examples cited.

FEDERAL PROGRAMS

There is no way to tally precisely the number of older Americans engaged in educating roles of all kinds, whether in institutions or in other organized programs or as individuals (church members, for instance). As noted earlier, a rough estimate would put the number at one million. Of these, less than 5 percent are enrolled in programs sponsored and administered by the federal government.

During 1976, eleven federal programs placed an estimated 42,000 adults 60 years of age and older in a broad range of educating roles in schools, libraries, day-care centers, museums, and other community agencies. Table C presents the numbers of such adults in the following pro-

TABLE C

Number of Older People (60+) Serving in Educational Roles Through Eleven Federally Administered Programs 1976

Number of local sites	Program	Number of older people in program	Estimated number of older people in educational roles
680	Retired Senior Volunteer Program/ACTION	210,000	15,000
182	Foster Grandparent Program/ACTION	14,157	11,326
n/a	Peace Corps/ACTION	131	131
598	Volunteers in Service to America/ACTION	312	53
7000	Head of Start/U.S. Office of Education	6,428	6,428
312	Service Corps of Retired Executives/Small Business Administration	6,624	6,624
3882	Green Thumb/National Farmers Union	5,597	785
65	Senior Community Employment Program/National Council of Senior Citizens	2,785	728
34	Senior Community Service Project/National Council on the Aging	1,252	227
62	Senior Community Service Employment Program/National Retired Teachers Association/American Association of Retired Persons	3,800	582
	TOTAL	251,086	41,884

Source: Academy for Educational Development, 1977

grams: the Retired Senior Volunteer Program (RSVP), Foster Grandparent Program (FGP), the Peace Corps, Volunteers in Service to America (VISTA), the Service Corps of Retired Executives (SCORE), Green Thumb, Head Start, and three Senior Aides programs operated concurrently by the National Council of Senior Citizens (NCSC), the National Council on the Aging (NCOA), and the National Retired Teachers Association/American Association of Retired Persons (NRTA/AARP), under contract with the U.S. Department of Labor.

Four of these federal programs are clustered under the umbrella of ACTION, the agency created in 1971 that "unites all the federal volunteer agencies into one single effort devoted to making life better for people the world over." Its best-known components—the Peace Corps and VISTA—actively recruit older men and women, though their participation in these organizations is minor. RSVP and Foster Grandparents, however, are designed specifically "to give retired people a meaningful opportunity to channel their talents into volunteer community service projects"; they recruit only adults 60 and over.

> *The Peace Corps.* From its start, in 1961, the Peace Corps has recruited older Americans. (Hardly anyone can be unaware that Miss Lillian, of Plains, Georgia, was a Corps-person in India in her late sixties.) The developing countries to which Peace Corps members are assigned value skills and talents that derive from life experience as much as they value formal credentials. Peace Corps volunteers teach, tutor, and counsel in everything from agriculture to calculus. In 1976, out of nearly 6,000 volunteers and trainees, there were approximately 101 aged 61 to 70, and 30 aged 71 and older. All of them worked in educational roles. While in training and during service, Peace Corps volunteers receive a monthly allowance for food,

travel, rent, and medical needs for an average annual expenditure of roughly $3,000 per volunteer.

VISTA (Volunteers in Service to America). VISTA recruits men and women of all ages to work for at least one year in impoverished rural and urban areas of the United States—with migrant families, on Indian reservations, in institutions for the mentally handicapped, in Job Corps centers. About one-quarter serve in educational settings. In 1976, about 9 percent of VISTA's 3,357 volunteers were 60 years or older—some 312 men and women.

In contrast to the few hundred older adults in these two ACTION operations, upwards of 225,000 men and women 60 years old and older are enrolled in two other education-related ACTION programs designed specifically to involve older people in a diversity of community services, some broadly educational.

The Foster Grandparent Program. FGP, which began in 1965 as a cooperative effort of the Office of Economic Opportunity and the Department of Health, Education and Welfare, was transferred to ACTION in 1972.

In 1976, FGP enrolled over 14,000 people in 182 local centers on a budget of $34 million (as against 4,000 people in 67 centers on a budget of $10.5 million in 1971). Foster Grandparents, most of whom are women, work four hours a day, five days a week, devoting two hours each day to each of the two children in their care. They receive a stipend of $32 a week, which is tax free, a transportation allowance, hot meals while on the job, accident insurance, and annual physical examinations.

The Foster Grandparents Program makes it possible for men and women age 60 and over, who are in good health, capable, and poor, to devote love and attention to physically, emotionally, and mentally handicapped children. The work, originally confined to institutions, now has been exetnded to private settings of various kinds.

All volunteers get 40 hours of orientation as well as training while they are in service; they are supervised by child-care specialists in their assigned agencies. Grandparents' tasks range from feeding and dressing the child to playing games and reading stories to speech and physical therapy. Evaluative studies of the program as a whole and of the development of the children involved have documented the value of FGP, even its cost/benefit.

The organization takes pride in any number of small success stories, in which the foster grandparent has made a signal difference in the life of some one child, sometimes freeing him or her from institutional life.

The Retired Senior Volunteer Program. The success of the Foster Grandparents program prompted many older Americans whose incomes exceeded the eligibility limit to write to their Congressmen and others about the need for a similar program they could take part in. As the result of this interest and of a successful pilot program in New York City, RSVP was authorized in 1969 and got under way two years later, joining ACTION in 1972. Like its predecessor, RSVP has grown rapidly—from 1,800 volunteers in 84 local projects and a budget of $5 million in 1972 to about 210,000 volunteers in 680 projects with a budget of $19 million in 1976.

Except for their focus on older people as community servants, RSVP and Foster Grandparents are very different. RSVP enrolls more than fourteen times as many people as does FGP on a budget more than $15 million lower. The discrepancy has several operative reasons. Senior Volunteers receive no stipend, though local sponsors sometimes provide lunches and transportation. Their hours of work, which vary according to local and individual needs, rarely match the twenty hours per week required of Foster Grandparents. Also, local sponsors share an annually increasing portion of the program's cost. ACTION considers RSVP "inherently a local program," since it is "locally planned, operated, controlled, and supported."

Senior Volunteers are given orientation but less sustained training than the Foster Grandparents. Finally, RSVP embraces a much wider spectrum of volunteer work. Local sponsors include schools, libraries, correctional institutions, hospitals, nursing homes, government agencies, and courts. Work encompasses everything from fixing toys to restoring antique planes to phoning shut-ins. Only an estimated 7 percent of the 210,000 Senior Volunteers work as teachers or in roles closely related. The educational roles are diverse, sometimes taking advantage of onetime avocations and leading to second careers.

An outside evaluation, made in 1973, showed that almost three fourths of the local RSVP sponsors found their Senior Volunteers a valuable supplement to their staffs; two thirds of them stated they would be forced to cut services or programs without them. Furthermore, the study found that their experience had not only improved the spirits and outlook of a full four fifths of the volunteers themselves, but that more than half of them also felt better physically.

Service Corps of Retired Executives. SCORE, sponsored by the Small Business Administration, brings the knowledge and experience of retired business managers to the owners or managers of small businesses and community organizations. Founded in 1964, SCORE has responded to over 500,000 requests for assistance—in accounting, finance, advertising, marketing, taxation, and other aspects of management. Some 6,600 older volunteers, working out of 312 SCORE chapters throughout the country, have aided a great array of enterprises, including grocery and drug stores, fast-food franchisers, repair shops, truckers, laundries, and small manufacturers. Out-of-pocket expenses are reimbursed, on request.

Head Start. This ground-breaking and often beleaguered program, run by the U.S. Office of Education, is marginally involved with the use of older adults. Out of more than 160,700 volunteer and paid employees working in Head Start's 7,000 local programs in 1976, only 4 percent (about 6,400 people) were 60 years old or older. Virtually all of them worked as teachers or tutors. Sometimes older persons participating in the Foster Grandparents Program or RSVP are assigned to Head Start programs.

In addition to these programs financed and administered by Washington, the following national programs, financed through the federal government but operated by private non-profit organizations, put older people to work at useful social tasks that include educational service. All together, these programs deploy only about 13,400 older adults—a fraction of those in the ACTION programs—with an estimated 2,300 of them working in educational capacities.

Green Thumb. The largest of the programs is Green Thumb. Sponsored and administered by the National Farmers Union, under a grant from the U.S.

Department of Labor, the program employs older, low-income people to carry out conservation and community-improvement projects. There are local branches in 31 states, plus the District of Columbia and Puerto Rico. To qualify, a Green Thumb worker must be at least 55 (the bulk of them are between 60 and 75), come from a rural background, receive an annual income below the poverty level, and pass a physical examination. Each worker serves an average of 20 hours per week earning an average wage of $2.68 an hour. Of the nearly 5,600 adults aged 60 and over participating in this program in 1976, roughly 780 were engaged in such educational jobs as teaching, serving as library aides, and working in Head Start projects and day-care centers.

Senior Aides. The Senior Community Service Employment Program, authorized by Title IX of the Older Americans Act of 1965, and administered by the U.S. Department of Labor's Office of National Programs, is designed to employ low-income older people in community service projects.

The Department of Labor has contracted with five national organizations to mount and operate local programs. Among these five organizations are: the National Council of Senior Citizens, the National Council on the Aging, and the National Retired Teachers Association/American Association of Retired Persons.* A specific set of communities and a specific number of job slots were assigned to each organization.

These three institutional contractors, with combined funding of just under $5.8 million at the start,

---

*The other two contractors are the National Farmers Union, whose Green Thumb program has been described, and the U.S. Forest Service.

had budgets totalling close to $62 million for fiscal 1978. Although the three programs differ slightly in their organization and administrative methods, their basic mandate, operation, and eligibility requirements are all but identical.

A prospective senior aide must be at least 55; income must not exceed the poverty level set by the Department of Labor ($2,970 a year in 1977); and he or she must be either retired or chronically unemployed. Potential aides take medical examinations to determine their capacity for regular employment. Once accepted, senior aides work 20 hours a week earning an average wage of $2.50 an hour. On the average, aides are upward of 65 and the majority never finished high school.

All senior aide programs operate through offices run by local project directors. The aides receive on-the-job training in community and public-service agencies for an unspecified period of time. Once trained, the aide may be hired by the agency in question, or be placed by the local project office with some other employer, public or private. Thousands of trainees have gone on to permanent jobs in great variety, some of them—day-care workers, for instance—related to education.

All three contractors agree that the success of the senior aides program depends to a large degree on the skill, patience, ingenuity, and persistence with which the local project director or his "job developer" scours the community for training/job opportunities and matches them to available aides. The best job developers are often senior aides themselves.

AN INTERIM SUMMING UP

According to the evidence of the foregoing pages on the deployment, nationwide, of older adults in educational roles:

1) A verifiable 100,000 or so are so engaged, most of them as unpaid volunteers, in a broad spectrum of jobs. There are undoubtedly multiples of this total working as teachers or in related educating capacities, especially if churches, corporations, and other settings not covered by the survey are included. There is reason to add at least another 900,000.

2) Whatever the true total, it clearly falls far short of the millions of older Americans—as indicated, for instance, by the Harris poll—who want to keep on working, would welcome training, and are equipped and willing to serve.

3) From the survey findings and from evaluations of federal or federally sponsored programs, it is clear that society and the children and adults who compose it are reaping rich benefits from the older people who are helping them to learn.

FOUR

A Record of Accomplishment: Some Cases in Point

Like any social phenomenon, the involvement of older people in educating roles is more readily grasped if generalities and abstractions are brought down to cases—especially as is true here, if the phenomenon has had limited recognition. Chapter Three presented a rough blueprint, from a nationwide perspective, of the scope and nature of adults' involvement in teaching or related activities. The 22 programs described here may stand as surrogates for perhaps several hundred programs in communities, large and small, across the country where older Americans help in the education of others.

One purpose of the present report is to suggest that these programs, in their diverse and independent ways, exemplify the value of an idea whose time has come.

The examples, while highly selective, are neither random nor arbitrary. They were chosen, as were the supplementary examples presented in Appendix D, to give some notion of the great range of possibilities embraced in the concept of older persons as educators—as to the kind of work done, the students served, the diverse backgrounds and capacities of the older educators, the settings and auspices of the programs they work in, the size and tenure of the programs.

- [ ] The instructional field ranges from crocheting to salesmanship to Greek drama to microbiology to swimming.
- [ ] The "students" range from nursey-school toddlers to nonagenarians, from Latin American farmers to fast-food franchisers.
- [ ] The educators range from law school deans and eminent professors emeritus to experienced housewives to dirt farmers to Hebrew scholars to union organizers.
- [ ] The settings include schools, prisons, nursing homes, senior centers, day-care centers, hospitals, military installations, graduate schools, settlement houses, banks, churches, private homes.
- [ ] The auspices can be anything from a single determined individual to the U.S. Government.
- [ ] Programs may involve only a few older persons or as many as 2,500. Some of them are one-shot efforts; others have been solidly established for years.

Like hundreds of other programs across the nation where older people act in teaching roles, few of the programs presented here have achieved fame beyond their immediate locale or their particular field. This relative invisibility has little to do with success or failure. Generally speaking, these programs have proved sucessful by almost any measure, pragmatic or spiritual, human or economic. If the results have not achieved appropriate renown, it may simply be that program directors are too preoccupied with the work at hand to publicize their successes.

EDUCATING THE YOUNG

School Programs

The school volunteer, once regarded as at best a pleasant but dispensable adjunct to education and often the object of professional suspicion, is here to stay.

In 1974 an estimated 5.5 million Americans volunteered their services to the nation's educational enterprise, according to Census Bureau data. Of these, some 3.5 million adults of all ages now take part on a regular basis in an estimated 4,000 organized school volunteer programs across the country, according to the National School Volunteer Program. The typical volunteer is still the parent (usually the mother) of school-age children. But increasingly she, or he, is working alongside men and women aged 60 or older who bring to the job a lifetime's experience in industry, the professions, the arts, or homemaking.

Beginning in 1974, special large-scale efforts to recruit, train, and place older adults in the public schools have been under way in Los Angeles, New York City, and Miami, supported by private foundation grants. Earlier, a similar project initiated in Winnetka, Illinois, served as a model for programs throughout that state.

The Volunteer Talent Pool: Winnetka, Illinois. One of the earliest experiments in the use of older school volunteers occurred in 1967 when the Winnetka school volunteer program, then known as Project for Academic Motivation (PAM), received a two-year grant from the Administration on Aging to conduct a special drive to recruit older adults. The drive was eminently successful. In 1968-69 more than 60 percent of Winnetka's school volunteer force was over age 55. The AoA grant also enabled a Winnetka team to help communities all over the state to develop similar programs.

Although PAM no longer exists in name, its practice of recruiting older volunteers has been taken over by community-run school volunteer programs in Winnetka and other suburban Chicago communities. Recruitment is now carried out by local Volunteer Talent Pools which in turn assign volunteers to schools that have appointed volunteer coordinators.

In Winnetka, where it all started, over 80 percent of the 1976-77 school volunteer force of 170 were persons 50 years of age and over.

For more than a decade this Illinois experiment has demonstrated that older adults in significant numbers are available and willing to help others learn, and that a project developed in one affluent, progressive community can be successfully adapted to communities and schools covering a wide socioeconomic stratum.

Dedicated Older Volunteers in Educational Services (DOVES). The Los Angeles Unified School District, the second largest school system in the United States, is second to none in the multitude and variety of learning problems and needs manifest in its 650 schools. For some fifteen years it has used volunteers in an effort to alleviate some of these problems. In the 1976-77 school year, out of a volunteer force of more than 20,000 adults, close to 2,500 were men and women aged 60 to 98. This was the outcome of a concerted drive to recruit older adults, under a challenge grant of $100,000 from a major foundation.

In 1974, with one year's prior experience in an experimental "Grandparents" program, the professionally staffed school volunteer program opened up a full range of opportunities to older adults, using the public relations staff of the school district, an expert in community relations as project director, and a staff of twelve part-time recruiters.

Responding to publicity in *The Los Angeles Times,* neighborhood newspapers, and television shows, older residents by the hundreds came forward—retired professionals, retired actors, retired business people, retired workers and homemakers. One retired executive of Hughes Aircraft wanted to help kids learn to read. A black grandmother who had only three years of schooling herself "knew how important it was to help children to be calm so they can learn." A doctor wanted to let youngsters know how badly they were needed in the health care system. A furniture company executive wanted to help handicapped children to learn furniture trades so they would not be a burden to society. A retired personnel executive, a woman, wanted to help a teacher in her record keeping as well as in supervising the class.

Endorsed by the Chamber of Commerce, the DOVES program gained wide support in business and industry. A Gold Ribbon Committee, including such celebrities as Nanette Fabray and Ricardo Montalban helped in recruiting and in developing community support for the program. Older volunteers were welcomed into any educational role that suited their interests and abilities. Most became tutors in reading, math, or English as a second language. Many aided playground, lunch, or bus supervision. Others served as classroom grandparents. Many helped with administrative tasks.

Noteworthy among the efforts by older volunteers has been their effective work with handicapped children. "These people really care," was the testimony of one teacher. And a program director noted, "Older volunteers know how important independence is, and the opportunity to help youngsters to achieve it despite handicaps was a challenge that captured their energy and commitment. The children responded and veritable miracles of development occurred."

The DOVES program, the largest in the nation using older school volunteers, expects to expand still further. The professional staff believes there may soon be 3,000 DOVES and even 4,000 eventually. Turnover is low. DOVES now serve in 600 of the city's schools, and program staff is confident that before long they will be serving in the remaining 50. The success stories stemming from the first three years of the DOVES program have created a growing demand for more such volunteers. Sustained funding remains a problem, though the program now gets some financial support from the school district and from other community sources.

During the 1976-77 school year, the school district conducted a six-month in-depth study of the results, in the 600 schools, of the use of DOVES and other volunteers. Interviews, consulations, and observation provided convincing evidence that the older volunteers were enhancing the quality of education in many ways. Among other things their assistance made it possible for the regular teachers to do a better job, and in general made possible greater freedom of movement, greater use of small groups, more enrichment, independent work, and individual teaching.

Similar programs have also been operating since 1974 in New York City and Miami, with results that have been equally satisfying if not quite so resounding numerically. By the end of the 1976-77 school year, some 995 older volunteers had been recruited to serve in 192 New York City schools, almost all of them as tutors. In the same period, Miami's Older Volunteers in Education (M.O.V.E.) had placed close to 1,000 older volunteers in 200 schools.

New York's Older Adult Program opened up a new possibility—the practice of forming a single group of volunteers from one corporation, say, or from a senior center, who travel and work together as a tutorial unit in a given school. A staff member pointed out that "this procedure has enabled us to service schools in poverty neighborhoods to which many volunteers are reluctant to travel alone." The Miami program, which recruited at close to 100 locations from flea markets to churches, found a way to use older volunteers who wanted to help but were unable, for physical or other reasons, to work in the schools. An additional 350 elders have made their contribution by developing hand puppets, educational games, and other materials at home.

Seniors Tutor for Educational Progress (STEP). With initial funding under Title III of ESEA, middle schools in exurban Connecticut have since 1973 run a promising program that links older persons with teenagers. Some 35 senior tutors work at schools in Redding, Middletown, and Monroe, tutoring students identified as having learning disabilities.

Materials they fashion with their STEP teenagers to help solve specific learning problems include stick figures, map distance games, cause-and-effect games, beat-the-band games. The tutors are paid $2.50 an hour, work four hours a day, and choose how many days they want to work per week.

Among them are a former fashion designer, a successful commercial illustrator, an Olympic swimming medalist, a specialist in preventive medicine, a department-store buyer and amateur musician, a school bus driver, and a specialist in metal alloys with close to half a century's experience in a steel company.

The senior tutors' ways of helping the children are as diverse as their backgrounds. One woman teaches grammar by means of an ingenious variation on bowling. The student rolls a whiffle ball the length of a cafeteria table towards plastic bottles set up as pins. Each bottle contains a slip of paper explaining the formation of a common contraction (or whatever). When he knocks over the bottles, the student checks their contents and presumably reinforces through the pleasures of the game his grasp of grammatical basics. Another tutor, a former librarian, has helped a boy who is a fresh-water fishing enthusiast to produce a book on the subject; a former professional artist among the tutors helped with the illustrations. As far as possible, STEP tries to match up the particular strengths of the tutor, whether vocational or avocational, with the particular needs and interests of the teenager.

At the start of the 1977 school year, the STEP program was adopted in nearby Brookfield and Newtown.

Teaching-Learning Communities (T-LC): Ann Arbor, Michigan. Among the country's various efforts to bring old and young together in the schools, T-LC is distinctive in its focus on the arts and crafts.

T-LC started in 1971 when Carol Tice, an elementary school art teacher, drove three older volunteers from school to school in her own car. Today the project, headed by Mrs. Tice, has a modest staff, including a number of paraprofessional aides, under a substantial development-and-evaluation grant from Title III (now IV-C) of ESEA. During 1975-76, the second year of federal funding, it operated by request in seventeen schools and involved 125 retired persons aged 60 or more.

In 1976-77, Ann Arbor children and their "grandpersons" worked together to complete 246 projects in: the visual arts, graphics, crafts, woodworking, carpentry, photography, film-making, pottery, weaving, rug-hooking, music, lace-making, movement, reading, storytelling, and such "environmental arts" as gardening, flower arranging, and plant care—to name a few. In addition there were "mini-courses" in a variety of fields including rocks, electricity, and Chinese language and culture. Children and elders played problem-solving games. They also heard and sang ethnic work songs.

T-LC's volunteers, who have ranged in age from 60 to 93, come from single dwellings, public housing, and retirement and nursing homes; they represent a broad diversity of ethnic, social, and occupational backgrounds. They receive no stipend, but RSVP supplies transportation as well as accident and liability insurance. Most of them spend half-day sessions at school, either once or twice a week. An effort is made to adjust the age and size of the student group, as well as the time and frequency of meetings, to suit each particular volunteer.

The external evaluation of T-LC, issued in August 1976, reported that: "1) Children are learning many and various art forms and experiences from grandpersons; 2) Grandpersons are capable of increasing the cognitive growth of children in subject-oriented experiences; 3) Children in the T-LC program positively perceive grandpersons as 'helpful,' 'good,' 'happy,' 'fun,' and as a teacher; 4) Parents are highly supportive of the program."

Initial funding was based on benefits to children. In 1977-78, however, the project will focus on how the learning needs of older persons themselves are also being met through T-LC.

Outside the Schools

Volunteers have always been the mainstay of programs for children and young people outside of school—in scouting, 4-H clubs, Little Leagues, community arts and recreation programs of all kinds. As in the schools, the typical volunteer for such after-school/weekend programs is still the parent with school-age young: here fathers figure prominently. But campaigns have been mounted to involve older adults in such work. One such example:

Expanded Horizons. Basket weaving, banjo-picking, flat-footing, crocheting; dried apple pies, molasses stack cake, split-hickory stool bottoms, caning, and apple butter; country history, chivaree, riving—these are some of the skills, arts, and products that opened up horizons in a pilot 4-H program conducted in six counties in southwest Virginia. Funded through Title I of the Higher Education Act of 1965 and administered by the Extension Division of

Virginia Polytechnic Institute, Expanded Horizons' prime purpose was to identify older Americans adept in traditional arts and skills, recruit them as 4-H club volunteers, and bring them together with interested young 4-H members.

According to the project director, the results were "almost unbelievable." From September 1975 through April 1976, Extension Agents and especially hired technicians recruited 763 older adults. In that period they worked with over 7,500 members of 4-H clubs in a variety of ways. Some came to club meetings and demonstrated their talents and crafts. Others just talked about how it used to be. Others led small groups or directed shows and public events. Some worked in their homes with one or two 4-H members on specific projects. Still others took pictures, kept records, and led singing.

By all accounts, everybody benefited from the experience. The young club members gained knowledge and skills, old crafts were revived, the older volunteers through this invigorating new relationship with the young found a fresh outlook on life. As for the Extension Agents and 4-H leaders, they found in the success of Expanded Horizons several useful implications for 4-H and other Extension programs. They were surprised, for instance, at the young people's enthusiasm for quilting, county history, old-time music and dance. They were impressed by how many older people would contribute their abundant knowledge and skills if they were properly approached. It took time to overcome initial diffidence and even suspicion on the part of the elders. "They wanted to know very specifically what was expected of them," project director Neel Rich reported. "They were reluctant to make long-term commitments. Many were willing to work only with small groups." An important finding: "When we recruit volunteers, we need to first identify particular talents which are needed, develop clearly defined expectations for volunteers, then recruit for these specific tasks."

EDUCATING ADULTS

Here we shall look at programs in a variety of settings that use older Americans, mostly but not always as volunteers, in the instruction of adults of college age and older.

In Colleges and Universities

At *Hastings College,* the University of California's law school in San Francisco, retired law professors have a chance to go on teaching as long as they like. Hastings has long sought out qualified law professors about to retire and invited them to move to Hastings, which offers a full professorship, salary, and privileges.

The college undertook its campaign more than 30 years ago when the Second World War created a professorial shortage, and has continued active recruiting ever since, so successful have been the results. Today a third of the faculty is 65 or over. Among the recruits over the years have been the former dean of New York University's law school and a former U.S. Supreme Court Justice.

According to Associate Dean Francis Seidler, "The idea of giving retired professors and deans an opportunity to carry out their activity as long as they like is unqiue. We have men who teach into their eighties, without interruption."

La Verne College: La Verne, California. In 1973, this small liberal arts college initiated a volunteer program of its own that uses retired people to work with students in various ways and to expand the curriculum. For this program, called "New Dimensions," retired residents of the area were asked to specify their "life experiences and areas of expertise" and to volunteer to work with college students as mentors. Leland Newcomer, then president of La Verne, acknowledged an initial lack of interest on the part of students, but by 1974 noted that "now it's starting to percolate. The more it works, the better it works."

La Verne College is fortunate in the number and quality of retired persons living nearby in an area of Southern California, where retirement communities abound. Among them are former professors and missionaries, several Nobel Prize winners, and members of many professions.

According to President Armen Sarafian, La Verne derives great academic advantages by "utilizing these people as special resources to enrich the normal classroom. A freshman class studying American government, for example, has the thrill of meeting with a former Congressman for a week to discuss the legislative process."

A bastion of volunteers for New Dimensions is an upper-income retirement enclave called Hillcrest Homes. A roster prepared in 1974 of Hillcrest residents organized by field of competence covered some fifty-odd specialties ranging alphabetically from Accounting to YMCA, and including—along with such standards as Biology, Engineering, Psychology, Greek, and Law—such unique entries as Air Conditioning, Euthanasia, Legal Work for American Indians, Medical Christian Mission, Motion Picture Publicity, and Noise Control.

The college offers no stipend to its many volunteers, but does provide meals and pays for certain expenses. As it happens, few of the retired people need or want monetary compensation. As former President Newcomer once observed, the volunteers "would rather take part in our program than eat."

The college has noted a happy by-product of New Dimensions since its inception in 1973. More and more older people are enrolling in La Verne classes, sometimes for credit. The college has set up a special program for older adults that allows them to pursue a degree they had long ago abandoned.

In Other Settings

Senior Volunteers for Monroe Reformatory. Senior Volunteers recruited through the RSVP program of Snohomish County are contributing to job training, rehabilitation, job development, tutoring, and other educational services at Monroe Reformatory, a Washington state prison. Some volunteers draw on their past experience to instruct inmates in such trades as meat cutting, horticulture, landscaping, and mechanics. Others counsel inmates who are soon due for release on job prospects and the world of work. These counselors see their "clients" once a month and spend considerable time developing jobs. After a man is released, the volunteer counselor keeps in touch with him and tries to ease the transition between prison and employment.

In addition, volunteers work at the Hill House Children's Center, a child-care service that operates during visiting hours at the reformatory. They also take part in tutoring. During most of the year, about 25 volunteers work one day a week at the prison. Volunteers get on-the-job training, and are viewed as members of the staff by Monroe officials.

In Business and the Professions

International Executive Service Corps (IESC). This nonprofit organization, based in New York, recruits experienced, usually retired, executives for short-term assignments as management advisors to locally owned firms and government enterprises overseas. Organized to help economic growth in developing countries, IESC has, since its founding in 1964, received close to $37 million in funding from the U.S. Agency for International Development, as well as financial support from some 300 major U.S. corporations and an equal number of overseas sponsors, many of whom are former IESC clients. Since January 1965, IESC volunteer executives have completed some 5,600 projects in 63 countries in Latin America, the Middle East, Southeastern Europe, Africa, South and East Asia. They have helped improve food producton and health care, textile and apparel manufacture, investment and banking practices, construction methods and transportation systems, industrial processes, merchandising and marketing programs, mining and natural resource development, government and educational services, and communications and tourist facilities. IESC pays travel and living expenses for the executive and his or her spouse, but no salary or fee of any kind.

Senior Medical Consultants (SMC). In 1965, Dr. Joseph Moldaver reached mandatory retirement age, and had to leave his post as associate clinical professor of neurology at Columbia University's College of Physicians and Surgeons. Soon after, he developed a plan whereby he and other retired clinical professors might have the option of resuming or continuing their work in a socially important way.

The result was Senior Medical Consultants, which began in 1970 as a pilot project with a two-and-a-half-year grant from the National Institutes of Health, and which made retired medical instructors available to community hospitals not affiliated with medical schools.

Having demonstrated its feasibility, SMC won major funding from the Bruner Foundation, and is now funded by other private foundations and by several corporations. Its board of directors and advisory council glitter with distinguished names. (Detlev Bronk was SMC's first President, from 1971 until his death in 1975.) Fully operational for seven years, the organization has a roster of about 125 "physician-teachers" whom it makes available to some 40 community hospitals, most of them in New York City and northern New Jersey, a few in Connecticut. Among them the teachers represent over 30 medical and surgical specialties. They offer both postgraduate work for interns and residents, and continuing education for hospital attending staff.

On the average, these "retired" physician-teachers work once a week or once a month, for sessions lasting from an hour to half a day. Some highly specialized practitioners may be called only for an occasional one-shot session. None of them receive more than token payment for their work. Hospitals, if they can afford to, pay a $100 fee for each clinical session (after evaluation by the institution, student doctors, and the teacher concerned). At present only four of the 40 participating hospitals make such payments.

In Dr. Moldaver's view, the purpose of SMC is to meet unfilled community needs in medicine and health care, not to keep old clinical professors busy. An SMC goal is to help each community hospital to become a small teaching center. One result of this emphasis is that about 20 percent of SMC's roster consists of younger physicians, attracted by the opportunity to teach in varied health-care environments and selected by SMC for their skill and experience, particularly in the newer medical specialties.

The success of the Senior Medical Consultants has generated enough publicity in professional circles to inspire four loosely affiliated offshoots—in Arizona, California, Florida, and Maine. SMC's long-term goal is to operate a national service. Meantime, accreditation by the American Medical Association has enhanced SMC's capability. Physicians can now receive credit for the SMC sessions they attend.

VITA (Volunteers in Technical Assistance). This lively and versatile organization has concentrated, since its founding in 1960, on helping people in the third world to solve their technical problems. To this end, VITA's small staff in Mt. Rainier, Maryland, directs a corps of 4,500 skilled volunteers, publishes manuals and technical bulletins, issues newsletters, and undertakes such special projects as adapting and testing various agricultural implements in Nigeria, helping a lime-producers cooperative in Honduras to develop a new kiln, and creating an "appropriate technology" center in Upper Volta. Increasingly wide recognition has come to VITA's leadership in the newly recognized field of appropriate technology.

At the core of all this activity are VITA's volunteers—scientists, engineers, architects, carpenters, agriculturists, educators, electricians, farmers. Over the years, the organization has responded to over 25,000 requests for technical assistance from all over the world, some through its available publications but most through direct participation by selected volunteers who correspond directly with the "requestor." Occasionally, if funds are available, volunteers make brief site visits.

Of all the volunteers on VITA's roster, an estimated 10 percent or more are retired. One of its most seasoned experts, an 86-year-old agronomist, was unable to attend a mid-1977 regional volunteer meeting in the United States because he was attending international conferences in Lepzig and Dublin. The organization has proved particularly suited to active people who want to contribute to third-world development but whose careers and personal responsibilities preclude their commitment for more than brief occasional periods.

"What we care about are a person's skills," Tom Fox, executive director, has said. "Age is irrelevant." There is, however, a decided advantage of age in VITA's work, according to Mr. Fox. "One of our volunteers farmed for 50 years in Kansas. In that span he experienced the transition from horse-and-plow to today's totally mechanized agriculture—a transition that developing countries are trying to encompass overnight. A man like this Kansas farmer can deal sensitively with the problems of change because he knows them first hand."

VITA's funding comes in approximately equal amounts from government and from private sources (individuals, foundations, and corporations). Volunteers receive no honorarium or stipend, except occasional reimbursement for out-of-pocket expenses. Full expenses are paid for on-site visits.

TEACHING PEERS

A logical and, it would appear, effective educating role for older Americans lies in teaching their peers, usually in a reciprocal teacher-student relationship. The potential of this kind of arrangement has barely been tapped, though as the examples below indicate, diversified models are available, including one New York City program now in its sixteenth year of successful operation.

The Institute for Retired Professionals (IRP). This well-known and widely emulated program, founded in 1962 at New York City's New School for Social Research by Hyman Hirsch, now the program's director, enrolls 600 members between 55 and 85, most of them retired doctors, dentists, lawyers, and teachers. For $250 a year a member is entitled to two credit courses chosen from the New School's curriculum (though few care about degrees) and participation in any number of 70 IRP courses—or groups as they are called. The roles of student and teacher are blended. As Hirsch has said, "We don't sit down and absorb. We are all teachers and students together." Rudi Goldsmith, for instance, a former exporter of textiles, teaches classical guitar and modern German literature as a group leader at IRP. Olga Kahn, at 75, leads a group in the novella and serves as poetry editor of the *IRP Review,* the Institute's glossy, student written and produced magazine.

Fromm Institute for Lifelong Learning. The Fromm Institute, recently established at the University of San Francisco, employs only emeritus professors to teach students aged 50 and over. When it opened early in 1976, the institute drew over 300 applicants but, because of limited funds, could accept only 75. Instructors are selected by a panel of local college presidents, which also reviews the curriculum. Courses, which tend to be broadly humanistic, included, during the first year of operation, such titles as "Value Systems in Milton's *Paradise Lost,*" and "Then and Now: a Comparison of the Last Century of the Roman Republic and the Twentieth Century."

The Institute of Study for Older Adults (ISOA). This diverse and ambitious program is run by New York City Community College and operates through the city's eight public community colleges. Besides enrolling adults from 60 to 104 years of age in courses given at over 100 locations all over the city, ISOA uses older persons in teaching roles and plans to use more.

In 1976, in cooperation with United Neighborhood Houses, the institute developed an educational program for elderly shut-ins. Arrangements were made for U.N.H. Senior Companions to attend ISOA courses; then, armed with course notes, materials, and TV assignments, the companions visited and taught their homebound clients. The response to the first two courses chosen, Home Gardening and Introductory Sociology, was "excellent," according to the institute.

In addition, ISOA recruited 25 older adults from its student body and brought them together twice weekly for nine weeks for an intensive course called "Techniques of Social Action." After completing this course, the institute reports, "these students returned to their centers to disseminate the knowledge they acquired to other elderly in their communities." Two of the students have become teachers in ISOA, which now includes twelve older adults on its faculty.

Senior Actualization and Growth Explorations (SAGE). SAGE was founded in 1974 in Berkeley, California, by several professionals from diverse disciplines who wanted to try out ideas they shared for revitalizing the lives and improving the physical and mental health of people over sixty. Towards this goal, the founders invited a dozen men and women in their sixties and seventies to join in an experiment that would test the applicability of a variety of techniques and disciplines for enhancing relaxation, self-confidence, balance, grace, mutual understanding, and self-image. Among them: deep breathing, biofeedback, autogenic training, massage, and the body movements of yoga and T'ai Chi Chuan. The results of this experiment gratified both young and old, teachers and students.

SAGE is essentially an adaptation of the human potential movement to the problems of aging and the elderly. It describes itself as "a program to alter negative ideas about aging, and demonstrate that people over 60 can grow, and transcend the expectations of our culture, to discover that old age can and should be a rich, creative culmination, involving as much growth as early childhood."

The idea for SAGE originated with Gay Luce, psychologist and writer *(Body Time, Sleep),* who seeing how meditation, relaxation, and other techniques had helped her 70-year-old mother, had looked in vain for the kind of program she might find of value when she herself grew old. Ms. Luce explored her ideas with Helen Ansley, then 74, whose favorable reactions encouraged the formation of the first SAGE group.

Not long after her introduction to SAGE, Mrs. Ansley's husband died and she moved to the Seattle area.

Besides leading a full social and community life, Mrs. Ansley, now 77, is team-teaching a SAGE class with young professionals at Bellevue Community College, coordinating the college's Holistic Health program, and working with a group in Seattle, "attempting to pass on to others the new image of aging that I gained through my SAGE experience."

Other "graduates" too have passed along SAGE's "new image of aging"—to residents of institutions as well as to new community groups of relatively healthy older people. In addition, they join SAGE staff in making presentations to such organizations as the University of California Medical Center, the California Association of Homes for the Aged, and San Francisco State University. A special outgrowth of the graduates' enthusiasm was their formation of an independent self-growth "community" in Berkeley to apply the SAGE experience to their lives.

Continuum Center, Oakland University: Rochester, Michigan. The Continuum Center for Adult Counseling and Leadership Training is, like SAGE, a product of this age of consciousness raising, but it is larger, longer established, and more institutionalized. Founded at Oakland University to assist adults in self-exploration, planning, and decision making, the center opened in 1965 as a women's center. It now serves men as well as women from young adulthood to old age—some 3,500 in its first ten years. Since 1972, the Continuum Center has offered group counseling programs for older people in cooperation with various community centers in the metropolitan Detroit area, and also trains a select group of these older people to be group leaders themselves. In the last few years the work with older people has so expanded that the center now has a separate Gerontology Unit, comprising both staff and older peer counselors.

Leaders of the Continuum Center's program for older people believe that "the value of peers as counselors has been demonstrated with varying populations, and may be especially important in dealing with older people." As they have observed, "It is difficult for clients to say that they are too old to learn when their group counselors range in age from 55 to 79, and are clearly launched in new directions."

PROVIDING SPECIAL EDUCATION SERVICES

Besides the educating roles illustrated above, there are others for which older adults qualify that are not readily pigeonholed. Here are a few diverse examples.

Senior Surrogate Parent Program: Miami. This one-year program, inaugurated in 1975 by the University of Miami's Community Development Division, offered instruction and on-the-job training in child care to elderly, unskilled workers, who then acted as substitute parents for young mothers so that they could go back to school or work. Funded by the Comprehensive Employment and Training Act (CETA), the program provided two weeks in the classroom and ten weeks on the job in homes and day-care centers. During this period the surrogate parents earned $2.30 an hour, and the families and day-care centers received their services free.

Of the initial 125 applicants, recruited primarily in low-income neighborhoods, 36 were chosen. All were at least 55, many over 60. Through discussion, films, and demonstrations on early childhood, the senior surrogates discovered ways to help young children learn and assess their development. Besides meeting the physical needs of infants, they learned to make toys from common household materials and watched videotapes of children's games. They studied ways to stimulate infants and ways to provide interesting play for older children. Trips to day-care centers gave them a chance to watch children at play and spot stages in child development.

According to the senior surrogates' young teacher, "They didn't just become baby sitters." The program had enthusiastic response from young mothers in the Miami area, a number of whom were happy to keep their surrogates on for pay after the ten-week on-the-job subsidized training period. Other surrogates have set up licensed day-care centers in their own homes or gotten jobs in day-centers. Once their training was completed, surrogate parents' work schedules varied. Some worked half days, some a few days a week, some every day, depending on employers' needs and budgets.

The program was suspended in September of 1976 when CETA funding was not renewed.

Legal Counsel for the Elderly. Legal Counsel for the Elderly began late in 1975 with an office in Washington, D.C., funding from the Administration on Aging, and sponsorship of the NRTA/AARP. Its purpose: to recruit and train senior volunteers for work as paralegals, under the direct supervision of attorneys, to provide free legal services in the area of public benefits to older persons.

Under this model project, District of Columbia residents 62 years of age and older, regardless of income, receive free legal help with programs such as Social Security, Food Stamps, Medicare, Medicaid, and Supplemental Security Income (SSI)—fields with which few private lawyers concern themselves, for obvious reasons. Assistance with wills and probate matters is also available for older persons with annual incomes of $8,000 or less.

Senior paralegals handle a majority of initial client interviews, and often are able to follow through with their cases, since most administrative hearings do not require the presence of an attorney. "As peers," Project Director Wayne Moore observed, "senior volunteers are able to bring an added dimension of compassion, understanding, and personal experience to their work with elderly clients."

The project's Washington, D.C. office, which handles an average of 60 new cases a month, as well as some 100 referrals and follow-ups on non-legal matters, operates with a shifting force of approximately 30 senior paralegals. Each paralegal serves a minimum of one or two days a week for three months.

A second phase of Legal Counsel for the Elderly, a

National Technical Assistance Program, was instituted in August 1976. Through this program, technical materials and staff support in the areas of senior volunteer recruitment, training and placement are made available to persons in each state charged by the AoA with the responsibility for developing legal services for older persons. In its first year the Technical Assistance Program provided training and other technical materials to legal service developers in 40 states, aided with recruitment of senior volunteers in 28 states, and ran paralegal training programs involving between 700 and 800 retired persons in 16 states.

Tax-Aides. This program of tax assistance for older persons by older persons was begun in 1968 by the Institute of Lifetime Learning, a continuing-education program of the NRTA/AARP. Since then it has grown into a free, nationwide tax counseling service described by financial columnist Sylvia Porter as "extraordinarily successful." In 1977 over 7,000 counselors helped an estimated 400,000 older people fill out their tax returns, in more than 1,500 communities across the country. During the "tax season" (January 1 to April 15), they set up for business in community centers, churches, banks, libraries, and other community locations.

To qualify as a tax aide, one must have a demonstrable aptitude for tax work. Volunteers receive two to three days special training from the Internal Revenue Service, and commit themselves to at least four hours of counseling a week during the tax season. Tax aides receive a stipend for each day of training they attend.

Language Bank, The City Hospital Center at Elmhurst, New York. This unusual service, which may have no duplicate anywhere in the country, was organized in 1974. Today upwards of 50 volunteers, mostly middle-aged to elderly, act as translators in twenty languages for patients being questioned by medical staff at the City Hospital Center at Elmhurst, which serves a large multilingual section of Queens in New York City.

The language bank can provide translators for: Arabic, Armenian, Chinese, Czech, French, German, Greek, Hebrew, Hindi, Hungarian, Italian, Korean, Polish, Rumanian, Russian, Serbo-Croatian, Spanish, Swahili, Tagalog (Philippines), Thai, Turkish, and Yiddish. Before the service was organized, staff members were on constant call to leave what they were doing and act as interpreters in the emergency room or the clinic.

To remedy this situation the director of volunteers, Emily Guttchen and her assistant, Patricia DeNigris, questioned the hospital's 350 volunteers about their language capabilities, and built up a card index of translators, with home phone numbers and information on times, including nights and weekends, they were available. The results have been excellent from every point of view. The translators have eased critical situations for patients and staff alike. They work with violent criminals in the psychiatric ward, patients whose larynxes have been removed and who can hardly speak, children and their mothers who are afraid of doctors and nurses. Sometimes the translator serves a function that transcends the easing of communication or abatement of fear. Irving Ozer, for instance, who is retired and who interprets Russian and Yiddish, rejoices in a patient he saved from what turned out to be an unnecessary operation, once Ozer cleared up the language barrier between patient and doctors. Zoe Ying Wei Ku, who translates Chinese, helped a speech pathologist determine that a patient, who had had a stroke, had made a considerable recovery in his speech and choice of words.

One translator, Ann Hicks, who is fluent in Spanish, French, Italian, and Portuguese, gave up a good job with a collection agency, where she had to convey threats to poor people. "I found the work obnoxious," she said. "I would rather do this for nothing."

FIVE

Future Directions for Older Educators

The programs outlined in this report represent a beginning. They stand as heralds of the day when, if good sense prevails, America's educational enterprise will take full advantage of this relatively untapped resource—the growing number of able, vigorous, experienced, and knowledgeable older adults.

To a large extent, the action recounted in these pages has been staged in the schools and colleges, in what is considered the traditional arena of education. However, as historian Lawrence Cremin reminds us in his new book, *Traditions of American Education,* the idea that education is confined to the schools is as recent as it is mistaken. Only in this century has "traditional" education been thus defined. We are now in the process of re-inventing the concept of education that prevailed until quite recently in our history. The identification of education with the schools, Cremin writes, "is increasingly replaced by a broader, more amorphous concept of 'learning,' which includes day care, parental behavior, television, adult education, and indeed all the significant places and ways in which efforts to promote human growth can occur." Among these many places are libraries, museums, hospitals, and workplaces of all kinds, including corporations. Concurrently schools and colleges are going outside their appointed confines of time, place, and curriculum to take advantage of diversified community resources and to meet the needs of mature and even aged students.

As these broader concepts of learning take hold, the opportunities for older adults in education will expand. In this section, we single out a few new directions and trends in education that may open doors to greater numbers of older educators. As the examples indicate, some of the ideas are already being tried. Others are still blueprints.

Trends in Elementary and Secondary Education

"By 2000," according to Wilson N. Riles, California's State Superintendent of Public Instruction, "it won't be necessary to go to high school every day. There won't be such a thing as a nine-month school. There will be year-round opportunities for learning, and the whole community will be the classroom." In these sweeping terms a highly unconventional state school superintendent encapsulates the movement to construe education as the function of the entire community—all kinds institutions and diverse people of all ages—and not just the function of the schools. The movement has manifested itself in many different ways in recent decades.

Career education, as it evolves, for instance, helps to break down school walls, letting children out and the world in. So do such efforts as the federally supported Artists-in-the-Schools program to make the arts come alive to young people in and out of school, through working with painters, poets, musicians, actors, and all manner of artists (age no barrier).

Superintendent Wilson Riles' plan for decentralizing control of California's schools, in which he has Governor Brown's backing, is the center of legislative controversy and widespread debate in the state. A first phase is now in effect. In 1975 the Early Childhood Experiment (E.C.E.) saw 43,000 parents and 37,000 volunteers help teach first-, second-, and third-graders everything from grammar to carpentry, under supervision by the regular classroom teachers. The state allocated $100 million directly to the participating schools, where so-called School Site Councils, with a minimum of state or local school-district interference, decide how to spend the money. (Councils are composed of parents, nonparents, and school staff, with parents in the majority.)

The system is designed to allow each school to allocate its funds where they are most needed. In a wealthy Los Angeles suburb, for instance, qualified parents volunteered to work full or part time in the classrooms to reduce the pupil-adult ratio. E.C.E. money thus could be spent for needed equipment, materials, or specialists. In poor neighborhoods, on the other hand, most of the money goes for paid paraprofessionals, since most qualified parents are otherwise employed. In between these extremes, schools have experimented with various combinations and recruited volunteer aides who are not parents—students from neighboring colleges who are preparing to be teachers, or older men and women. Reactions to E.C.E.'s first year were, for the most part, positive. According to one program coordinator, "the kids are just flying along in their studies," primarily, in his view, because "in E.C.E. there is less chance of failure because of highly individualized approaches."

If California's experiment toward uniting schools and community grows to include the whole school system, and the experiment catches on in other states, the use of older adults as resources and teacher aides can increase substantially.

Trends in General Adult Education

Adult education is not what it used to be, a melange of sometimes perfunctory offerings by school districts and university extension departments, correspondence schools, and other outposts of "real" higher education. Its preferred name today is continuing or lifelong or even "recurrent" education. At present, institutions of higher learning—especially the booming community colleges—have gone far beyond the reach of the old-time night schools and are responding to much broader constituencies. The concept of postsecondary education is changing, the definition of "student" is changing, content and methods are slowly changing to match. Opportunistically, in part, to compensate for the falloff in their traditional market of college-age students, traditional institutions of higher learning are devising newly flexible and diversified educational fare for a thronging new market of middle-aged housewives, mid-career executives, ambitious working people, convicts, the handicapped, and more and more, retired people and other older adults who want to learn.

With this striking shift in the focus of traditional higher education, it is no wonder that the contemporary adult student is finding a wealth of new or newly appreciated non-institutional ways to learn in what Ronald Gross in his book, *The Lifelong Learner,* calls the "Invisible University." Some of these ways are peculiarly adapted to the needs of the older learner, and to the aptitudes and capacities of the older teacher or mentor or counselor. Best of all, especially for older people, many of these educational modes combine the roles of student and teacher in a reciprocal relationship.

One of the newest inventions under the educational sun is the learning exchange, which resembles the free university that sprang up in the Sixties but is much freer in form. Instead of courses, the learning exchange offers a matchmaking service—matching up people who want to learn a particular thing with people who can and will teach it. Since 1972, an estimated 50 of these exchanges have been set up in communities and on campuses across the country. Their model is The Learning Exchange of Evanston, Illinois, which since its founding in 1971 has brought together some 50,000 teachers and learners to work on almost every imaginable subject from foreign languages, the sciences, and other academic standards to specialities like violin playing, plumbing, and fashion design to such outlandish subjects as clowning, fire eating, and fox hunting. Evanston's enrollment has included people of all kinds and colors and educational backgrounds, with ages ranging from ten to deep in the eighties. An 86-year-old woman has taught German to a young teacher planning a trip abroad. A retired sociology professor has taught French to four teenagers, who in return took care of her vegetable garden.

Another variation on matchmaking is the new practice called educational brokering. Modeled in general on the ground-breaking Regional Learning Service of Central New York, over 200 such agencies around the nation help adults plan and carry out their custom-made education, often keyed to careers. Through the service, adults of all ages are directed to appropriate sources of learning, whether in formal insituations or in any of the array of nonformal sources of education—Y's, proprietary vocational schools, churches, correspondence schools, and so on. The role of the counselor or consultant is crucial in the success of this new kind of service.

As adult education breaks loose from its onetime limitations of site and scope and more closely approximates "lifelong learning," it seems evident that older Americans will be in growing demand to contribute their knowledge and experience as teachers and counselors and mentors.

Trends in Industry-based Education

According to a study made by the Conference Board and

financed by the Carnegie Corporation and the Rockefeller Brothers Fund, the nation's 7,500 largest companies in 1975 spent more than $1.6 million for the "in-house" education of their employees—an estimated 3.7 million of them. These programs concentrate on upgrading the skills of employees or on teaching them new ones. As the *Carnegie Quarterly* observes, "Education in industry has become one of the fastest-growing educational enterprises in the country, and yet so little is known about it that it has been called 'a shadow education system.'"

One of the unknowns is the extent to which this huge system makes use of older or retired employees as teachers, a question the Conference Board report leaves unanswered. As the *Quarterly* noted, industry's greatest advance in its educational work has been in "making learning and knowing one continuous blend. 'Show-and-tell' classroom courses have given way to 'learning-by-doing from those who have done it,' to learning right on a production line, to learning in the lab or in the executive suite." According to the survey, major corporations employ about 45,000 persons full time on their training staffs. Carnegie believes that the findings provide "a starting point for thinking about ways in which these resources may serve the learning needs of the individual and society."

Already many companies are encouraging their employees, retired and otherwise, to work in such educational endeavors as school volunteer programs of various kinds. It would seem logical that industry might extend the use of older adults, especially a company's own retired employees, in its own vast, highly pragmatic educational enterprise.

Trends in Career Education

Whether "career education" as advocated in the Seventies is a new concept or a new name for an old concept is still a matter for controversy. Whatever one's special view, however, there is general agreement that vocational education, as commonly practiced, has been seriously deficient, and that a palpable need exists to acquaint students (the younger the better, some would say) with career options and to make truly effective training available when appropriate.

In his book *The Boundless Resource,* Willard Wirtz proposed to enlist the experience and judgment of the elderly in community councils that would guide people of all ages in decisions about careers. These councils would impart sophisticated up-to-date information, closely keyed to actual practice in local and regional industries (thus counteracting a widely acknowledged flaw of much vocational training); direct people to suitable education; and cut down the number of people trapped in disagreeable or boring jobs. It was Wirtz's hope to mount five-year experiments in twenty communities or so, at an estimated cost of $250,000 per community.

In New York City, the organization called Open Doors has for some years conducted a program, Lawyer in the Classroom, which provides lawyer volunteers to work with students and teachers in the public schools on a range of law-related topics from First Amendment freedoms to juvenile justice. In 1977 Open Doors introduced a new program, Business Person in the Classroom, which operates in the same fashion and offers topics from The Stockmarket to Business and Ecology. Though Open Doors has made no special effort to recruit older executives and lawyers, the opportunity seems obvious. What is also obvious is that this idea of seminars conducted by older experts is one that can be extended to a whole range of fields beyond law and business and can be adapted to virtually any educational setting.

As in other aspects of education, the key in good career education is to break down conventional barriers and to effect good working collaboration among schools, business, unions, and other germane institutions, as well as among people of all ages—those who would learn and those who can teach.

That older adults should be called upon more and more to add their weight of experience and knowledge to this endeavor is patent.

Trends in Second-Career Education

A recent phenomenon in the world of work has been the impulse of men and women in mid-life to change careers. The best-publicized individual examples are highly dramatic—from corporation president to minister, from engineer to sculptor, from C.P.A. to boat builder. To accommodate this growing movement, which has now enlisted many older persons, universities and other formal and nonformal educational institutions are trying to introduce new kinds of training and counseling programs or to refine existing programs. To pull together private and public efforts to aid older people who want to retire, not from the workforce, but from their usual employment, the American Management Association established, in 1976, a National Center for Career Life Planning. Through conferences, workshops, and research the center is dedicated to "serving the needs of the aging in America" with expert, specific guidance in moving to second or third careers.

In California, New Career Opportunities began operations in 1977 with a pilot project in Los Angeles. The program, which has foundation support, is modeled on the successful Junior Achievement model, and directed by a founding executive of that organization. Designed for men and women "who have retired or have been retired from the work force or have not been employed for some years," the program helps pople who are eager to put their abilities and experience to work. The goal is to encourage them to go into cottage-type businesses for themselves, built on their individual skills or hobbies. The learning device, as in Junior Achievement, is the establishment of "mock" companies by a dozen or so student members, with counseling by experts on all phases of starting and operating a business. Unlike Junior Achievement, however, the experts provide counseling and follow-up to the students as they go on to start up actual businesses of their own. According to director, Mike Parker, "our motto is to think small, because our purpose is to supplement fixed income, not make anybody rich, and I guess to have a little fun doing it." Within a year the program will be extended throughout Los Angeles County.

A nationwide Skills Matching Service was proposed some time ago by Robert N. Butler, director of the National Institute on Aging and winner of a Pulitzer Prize for his book *Why Survive? Growing Old in America.* Dr. Butler would have each community establish a computerized Skills Matching register to serve as a clearinghouse for all information on both jobs and services for the elderly. The program would, as he envisioned it, emphasize training designed to augment an older person's experience with needed new skills. It could also provide a means to preserve craftsmanship by locating the artists and artisans equipped to transmit the requisite skills. Dr. Butler believes that such a service is needed even where opportunities for paid or volunteer work already exist, since "existing employment services for the aged are most inadequate."

A limited application of this idea has been undertaken in Whitewater, Wisconsin. In early fall, 1977, the Committee on Aging at the University of Wisconsin's Whitewater campus instituted a Talent Bank of specific skills and expertise among older people willing to act as resource persons. Collaborating in the endeavor were the County Commission on Aging, senior centers, churches, and service clubs in the area.

For reasons that this report has documented, the use of older adults themselves as trainers and counselors in second-career education should increase along with the movement itself.

Trends in Education for Older Adults

Clearly, many of the education trends already highlighted suggest growing opportunities for adults equipped and willing to undertake educating roles in their later years. A particularly promising arena is the institution—center, institute, emeritus college—specifically designed *for* the education of older Americans. The number of such centers is growing apace. All are self-contained units within a larger university setting, and all confine admission to older adults; some set the entering age at 50 or 55, a few at 40.

Besides the special courses and other learning projects designed exclusively for the older student body, the students are usually encouraged (sometimes required) to extend their learning beyond the center itself. Almost always the students get the benefit of social and cultural extras in the host institution or community. Some centers include job counseling and placement in their services. The educational fare is predictably diverse, and varies from center to center. It may include pre-retirement education of all kinds (social, financial, psychological); practical and professional education; the liberal arts and sciences.

Most of the work tends to be noncredit (though a surprising number of older adults, some of them *very* old, seek credits and even go on to take advanced degrees). In general, the various centers admit anyone who meets the age qualifications regardless of previous academic or professional experience. An exception is the institute or center that builds its program around an enrollment of older adults able and willing to both learn and teach, as for example, the Institute for Retired Professionals at New York's New School for Social Research, and the Institutes for Learning in Retirement at Duke University and at Harvard. Such programs usually require something in the nature of a "suitable educational background."

In 1977 Duke University, a leader in the booming field

of gerontology, opened their Institute for Learning in Retirement, designed for retired professionals interested both in teaching and learning. For an annual base fee of $96, members take part in one institute course and one other learning experience, such as a course at the University itself. Included in a member's privileges is permission to audit any of Duke's undergraduate courses and unlimited use of library and cafeteria. Required of each member is some contribution each term to the institute's program, which these retired professionals help to design. A directorate of its own members administers the institute. A major part of the program is counseling members "in planning opportunities to put life experiences to practical use in local activities and social causes."

Also new in 1977 is Harvard University's Institute for Learning in Retirement, open to men and women who have retired from positions of responsibility in education, law, medicine, the arts, business and industry, government, and science, as well as to others who wish to pursue serious studies. The core of the program is the study group, which operates on a volunteer peer-teaching basis. Each group is formed of members sharing a common scholarly interest; each member is at once student and teacher, and shares responsibility for conducting seminars and discussion groups and for presenting papers. Membership, covering the institute's program and a wide range of social and cultural opportunities, costs $150 for the academic year. Included for no further charge is the privilege of choosing two courses a a year from the 200-odd courses offered by Harvard's Extension program and the new (noncredit) Center for Continuing Education.

Though all the likely trends in education today favor the greater use of older adults in teaching or similar educational roles, none seems more natural or fitting than the deployment of these older Americans in helping their peers to learn. Particularly promising is the fastest-growing segment of education for older adults: the university-based program whose participants reciprocally teach *and* learn, while themselves determining the nature and mode of the educational fare.

SIX

Guidelines for Program Development

Research findings and observations yield certain basic principles common to the best of the programs in which older adults have been recruited to serve the learning needs of others.

☐ **Start with the demand.**

Those programs work best that start with the problem (i.e. a specific educational need) and then recruit older men and women with the appropriate qualifications. *In the process* such programs enhance the self-esteem, dignity, happiness, and occasionally the income of the new "educators." To reverse this order, however—to say, "Let's find something for these bored and idle people to do"—is apt to produce a pseudo-program, one that benefits neither side of the equation.

In rural Virginia, for instance, Expanded Horizons first determined what young 4-H members were interested in, and *then* recruited those particular older persons adept at country music and dance, knowledgeable about local history, or skilled at one or another craft that the young people wanted to learn. In the New York City area, and in four other locations across the country, Senior Medical Consultants calibrates a select supply of retired clinical professors to the particular demands of community hospitals.

☐ **To attract and retain older workers, devise an appropriate strategy.**

Don't wait for older adults to volunteer. The initiative must come from the institution or group that is seeking qualified elders. A publicity release is not enough. One big-city YMCA, responding to the AED questionnaire, indicated it had made no use of older adults in any educational capacity in the previous year but noted: "We'd like to have them, but no one drops by." To be sure, every community has its share of men and women whose volunteer work after 65 makes no break with the past and who will simply continue or extend what they have been doing all along, or who have enough self-confidence and drive to undertake new ventures now that they have relinquished full-time responsibilities. Such exceptional people may well play a leading role themselves in initiating good programs for their less experienced peers. More typically, however, the potential worker among older people needs to be actively solicited.

Do not overlook the importance of compensation. Most older adults, as the Harris poll showed, respect the idea of volunteer work. By overwhelming majorities, people 65 and over agreed that such work was a good way for people to keep themselves busy and active, that it was "essential to meet the community's needs," and that "people with unused skills and talents should make use of them by doing volunteer work."

Despite these prevailing views, the survey revealed considerable reluctance among all age groups toward *doing* volunteer work. More than three quarters of the public 65 and over, and nearly as many under 65, agreed that "if someone's work is valuable, he should be paid for it." Moreover, the poll revealed negative feelings toward volunteer work for reasons other than economic. A full one third of older people agreed that "most jobs saved for volunteer workers are routine and boring, and not very rewarding."

These somewhat paradoxical findings contain several lessons for organizers of programs. One is that there will always be some people who cannot be drawn into unpaid, volunteer work whatever its attractions. Focus then, on the individual workers, or *kinds* of workers, your program needs, who are apt to be responsive to the work that needs doing. Some of these people, getting along on small fixed incomes from Social Security and perhaps other sources, simply cannot afford to work for nothing. Though they would willingly put in part of their days as volunteers, they may need modest stipends—recompense for transportation, meals, other out-of-pocket costs. Some of them might be satisfied by suitable payments-in-kind—training or course work that is satisfying in itself or that might lead to more substantial, perhaps paying, jobs. Others, somewhat better off and eager to stay active and use their knowledge and experience, would be glad to return occasionally to the university, hospital, or corporation where they once worked and, for an honorarium, conduct a lecture or lead a seminar. If, as occasionally may happen, a program needs a particular worker who must have a regular paycheck, it would be desirable to budget for this contingency.

Another lesson from the Harris survey is obvious: To attract and retain recruits, program directors must make sure that the work is not "routine and boring," that is is solid, productive, and rewarding—and so perceived on all sides.

Finally, all workers need proper *recognition* of their work—from their colleagues, their superiors, the general public. This recognition must be real. Even as a press release is insufficient to generate streams of volunteers, so also it takes more than a perfunctory pat on the head or form letter to retain them once recruited. Retention, a major problem in running volunteer programs, is further reinforced if the volunteer gains real social benefits from working alongside admirable people and from belonging to an organization that serves a valuable purpose.

☐ **Organize carefully to achieve good results.**

This blanket admonition embraces a number of highly important considerations. Good programs take account of them all.

Leadership. Exemplary programs are run by enthusiastic, able, and committed people, whose concern with both the program's purpose and its older workers is genuine, imaginative, and venturesome.

Coordination. Once a school, college, museum, corportation, service club, or ad hoc educational group has decided to enlist older workers for specific tasks, the program must be carefully coordinated and supervised. The most frequent complaint leveled against volunteer programs is their lack of organization. If volunteers don't know precisely what to do or what is expected of them, they tend to lose interest and to treat their schedules and assignments permissively. A volunteer's personal commitment is not enough. He needs the encouragement, guidance, and recognition that a well-coordinated, well-run program can insure. Implied here is supervision that is not oppressive or condescending, and on-the-job training as required.

Preparation, training, and acceptance. This aspect of programming comes in two parts: preparation of new recruits and preparation of the sponsor's regular staff—whether teachers, librarians, curators, or other professionals. Take school volunteers, for instance. Traditionally the classroom has been the sacrosanct domain of the teacher. Traces of suspicion toward volunteers still linger among teachers and their organizations, though it has much abated—partly because of the helpfulness volunteers have demonstrated, partly because bad times and crowded classrooms have made their help increasingly welcome. To make sure that older workers are well received, programs should involve permanent staff in preparing for them and in helping to design their tasks.

Even when assignments have been geared to individual talents and temperaments, many older workers need careful and gradual induction into their new roles. The nature and extent of this preparation will depend on both volunteer and program. The newly retired executive or professional may need little more than an introduction to the program at hand, unless it differs markedly from what he or she has been doing for a living. At the other extreme, those requiring the most patient preparation are older Americans who have been long retired from the workplace, have never worked for a living, or are quite diffident—as many older people are—about their capacities, talents, and general acceptance.

The directors of Virginia's Extended Horizons program found that their older teachers required "more time initially to develop their confidence and a little more follow-up." The same point emerges from other programs involving older Americans in educational roles for which previous experience provided little precedent.

The NRTA/AARP, when it began hiring senior aides for paid, part-time community service jobs, found that "it did not take many weeks for project directors to learn that it was going to take an average of three hours' time to fully hear and process a project applicant." The recruits needed counseling, sometimes over several days, and reassurance about such fears as losing Social Security benefits. According to the program's directors, in more cases than not the effort paid off.

The kind and extent of actual job training will also depend on the nature of the work to be done and of the older recruits. Recruits for Senior Medical Consultants, say, or for LaVerne College's New Dimensions require little more than nominal introduction to the mores and specific needs of the clients they will serve. The point is even more valid when it comes to corporations that enlist their retired executives or skilled workers for in-house training programs.

Recruits for school volunteers, on the other hand, will need something more, with emphasis on collaborative understanding between them and permanent staff. Much more elaborate training is required for work that recruits are learning almost *de novo*, like the peer counselors in Oakland's Continuum Center. Training older adults to serve as trainers of their peers has proven to be particularly effective.

Evaluation. There is an unfortunate tendency to view evaluation as something done after the fact—as an exercise in justifying expenditures of time, effort, and money. The use of evaluation merely as self-defense, however, short-circuits its most valuable role—that of a self-help tool for program directors and staff. Essentially, the purpose of evaluation is to document or discover the degree to which actual practice is accomplishing the goals and missions originally set for the program. For evaluation to best serve this purpose, it must be an integral part of initial program planning. Evaluation is a cyclical process, consisting of five major phases:

1) establishing program goals (what do you want the program to achieve?);
2) determining the kinds of specific objectives that will accomplish those goals (how can you reach the goal?);
3) creating methods of measurement to provide the kinds of information (data) that will indicate what progress, if any, has been made toward the goals you have chosen;
4) collecting the data (taking the measurements) and analyzing its implications (is practice measuring up to intent?); and finally,
5) using the findings to reappraise, and if necessary revise, those practices which appear ineffective in reaching your goals.

By this process of evaluation, a program administrator can continually correct his/her course toward the goals he/she has set out to reach.

☐ Financing.

Even a program staffed entirely by volunteers is not cost free. Money is needed for the administrative costs of recruitment, coordination, and supervision, in some cases for materials. As noted earlier in these guidelines, a program may need to make provision for monetary compensation of its older workers when indicated.

If good programs are to spawn others, it will be necessary to allocate funds for evaluating results of the program and for spreading the word. Some of the programs sampled in Chapter 4 have had the benefit of hundreds of thousands of private foundation dollars. Others have been subsidized in whole or part by public funds. Ideally (and it has happened in some of these programs) once the pump is primed, a successful program will gain permanent support from its institutional sponsor.

SEVEN

Conclusions and Recommendations

CONCLUSIONS

☐ Hundreds of thousands of older Americans are helping other people, of all ages, to learn, in many different kinds of educational settings both formal and nonformal.

☐ The vast majority of these older educators serve as part-time, usually unpaid, volunteers. They come from a wide spectrum of educational, socioeconomic, and occupational backgrounds, and serve in an equally diverse range of educating roles.

☐ The educational work these older people are doing is rarely makework. On the contrary, it is work that critically needs doing and that often would go undone without nonprofessional help.

☐ At present, the majority of educational and education-related institutions use at least a few older adults in educating roles. The average number per institution is low.

☐ These older educational workers get high performance ratings from administrators, professional staff, and students of all ages

☐ The Harris report discovered that an additional large, if indeterminate, number of well-qualified older persons would also be willing to help others to learn, if only they were asked.

☐ Demographic projections indicate not only that the proportion of older persons in the population will continue to rise, but also that these older people will be increasingly better educated, healthier, and more financially secure.

☐ At the same time, demographic developments are sharply modifying the size and composition of the traditional student body. As the number of students of conventional school and college age decreases, present trends suggest that the nation's educational enterprise will reach out to millions more students among the adult population and make use of more and more community resources.

☐ These trends pose the probability of ever-increasing opportunities for the effective use of older adults in educating roles.

☐ Programs organized to encourage the use of older people in meeting specific educational needs are achieving excellent results. Such programs have demonstrated the soundness of the proposition that older persons constitute a valuable educational resource.

☐ There are still not nearly enough of these well-organized programs, however. Nor have they been sufficiently publicized. Most of the programs are little known outside their immediate communities or fields of interest. As a result, the very concept of older persons as teachers is little appreciated by most educators, policy makers, and the general public.

☐ Despite the impressive achievements of programs that match the skills and experience of older adults to educational needs, their impact on the total educational enterprise or on the lives of most older people has thus far been minimal.

RECOMMENDATIONS

I. Public policy should encourage and promote opportunities for older people to contribute to the educational enterprise.

☐ Governmental and private grant-making agencies and institutions should increase these opportunities by soliciting proposals for projects designed to use the talents and abilities of older adults in general, or of particular groups of older people, to address specific educational needs.

☐ State departments of education and boards of regents should examine various incentives, financial and otherwise, that will encourage the regular use of qualified older adults in educational programs at all levels of the state's educational system.

☐ Municipal authorities should encourage the recruitment, training, and placement of older citizens in educational roles in such community institutions as libraries, parks and recreation departments, museums, community centers, health care institutions, as well as local schools and colleges.

II. Institutions, agencies and organizations concerned with education, formal and nonformal, should expand the use of older workers in educating roles, should provide adequately for their training and for the recognition of their accomplishments, and should provide the leadership and staff prepara-

tion necessary to support the involvement of these older workers.

☐ Information programs for educators need to be mounted at all levels within the educational community —from individual staff workshops to large-scale publicity by national associations—to increase awareness of the value of the educational services that can be provided by older persons, the widespread availability of talented and willing older adults, and of their proven ability to enhance the work of professional staff.

☐ Both preparatory and in-service training programs for professional educators and administrators should include courses in the management, coordination, and supervision of older part-time educational workers as members of an educational team.

III. Efforts should be made to collect, evaluate, and disseminate data and information about programs that are successfully using older adults in educating roles so that more and more communities are encouraged and guided in creating similar programs of their own.

☐ Program directors should themselves make an effort to inform others about their achievements and findings.

☐ National associations of educational institutions, education-related organizations, and older-adult membership organizations should consider joint sponsorship of an information clearinghouse that would serve simultaneously as a repository of research data and descriptive materials, and as a publisher of general and technical information serving the media and the public as well as governmental and educational agencies.

Appendices

APPENDIX A

SURVEY SAMPLE AND RESPONSE

	Sent	Responded	Percent of categorical responses	Percent of total response
FORMAL EDUCATIONAL INSTITUTIONS	3,346	1,097	32.8%	34.6%
Public school districts serving 5,000 or more students	2,136	547	25.6	17.4
Two-year colleges	568	236	41.5	7.5
Senior colleges and universities	598	306	51.1	9.7
Institutes of Lifetime Learning	44	10	22.7	.3
NONFORMAL EDUCATIONAL ORGANIZATIONS	8,152	2,046	25.1	65.4
Museums with designated education directors	94	70	74.5	2.2
Senior centers and clubs	1,912	334	17.5	10.6
Public libraries	1,327	212	16.0	6.8
Jewish community centers & YM-YWHAs	176	45	25.6	1.4
YWCAs	398	124	31.2	4.0
YMCAs	1,820	354	19.5	11.3
4-H clubs	2,425	907	37.4	28.8
ALL INSTITUTIONS AND ORGANIZATIONS	11,498	3,145	27.4%	100.0%

Source: Academy for Educational Development, 1976

APPENDIX B

Statistical Tables from the 1976 AED Survey of Older Adults as Providers of Education

TABLE 1

Average Number of Older Adults in Educational Roles at 2,426 Institutions

Type of Institution or Organization	Average number of older adults per institution
School districts	35*
Two-year colleges	12
Senior colleges and universities	8
Institutes of Lifetime Learning	33
Museums	16
Senior centers and clubs	33
Public libraries	7
Jewish community centers & YM-YWHAs	30
YWCAs	15
YMCAs	9
4-H clubs	21

*This figure represents the average per school district, *not* per school.

Source: Academy for Educational Development, 1976

TABLE 2
Fifteen Most Common Educational Roles Older Adults Perform at 2,426 Institutions

Role	Percentage of older adults	Number of older adults
Activity or project leader	23.1%	11,888
Resource person or special lecturer	17.6	9,048
Teacher	15.3	7,893
Tutor	12.1	6,235
Group leader	9.4	4,837
Educational advisory committee member	4.6	2,370
Teaching aide	4.5	2,338
Library aide or librarian	3.4	1,746
Curriculum consultant	2.1	1,100
Counselor	1.2	635
Administrator of education program	1.2	617
Media production staff member	1.1	575
Creator of educational games & classroom aids	1.0	535
Researcher	.9	462
Tour guide or docent	.6	291
All other	1.9	979
TOTAL	100.0%	51,549

Source: Academy for Educational Development, 1976

TABLE 3
Percentages of Older People in Educating Roles by Type of Institution

Type of Institution	Activity or project leader	Resource person/ special lecturer	Teacher	Tutor	Group leader	Educational advisory committee member	Teaching aide	Library aide	Curriculum consultant	Counselor	Administrator of an education program	Media production person	Creator of educational games & classroom materials	Researcher	Tour guide or docent	Other
School district	*	22	10	36	1	*	14	9	1	*	*	*	4	*	1	2
Two-year college	1	27	32	3	1	4	10	3	7	2	3	*	*	3	1	6
Senior college or university	1	17	40	5	1	2	3	6	7	2	10	1	1	3	1	5
Institute of Lifetime Learning	4	7	19	1	42	10	1	1	4	1	*	2	1	9	1	6
Museum	16	20	11	4	5	1	*	3	*	2	1	3	1	1	27	5
Senior center or club	25	21	19	4	16	7	1	*	2	2	*	3	1	1	1	*
Public library	7	17	5	5	2	1	1	27	*	*	*	12	1	3	5	16
YM-YWHA or Jewish community center	21	18	22	4	14	13	1	2	4	1	*	1	1	*	1	*
YWCA	27	15	19	5	14	10	*	1	2	2	*	2	1	*	1	3
YMCA	19	17	12	4	12	9	1	1	3	3	*	4	1	1	1	14
4-H club	49	11	13	2	15	7	1	1	1	1	*	*	*	*	1	*

*less than 1 percent

Source: Academy for Educational Development, 1976

TABLE 4
Percentage of Institutions Reporting the Use of Older People by Role and by Type of Institution

Type of Institution	Activity or project leader	Resource person/ special lecturer	Teacher	Tutor	Group leader	Educational advisory committee member	Teaching aide	Library aide	Curriculum consultant	Counselor	Administrator of an education program	Media production person	Creator of educational games & classroom materials	Researcher	Tour guide or docent
School district	*	54	40	52	—	1	38	33	11	5	13	2	4	3	—
Two-year college	—	43	69	13	—	4	11	15	26	10	21	*	1	7	—
Senior college or university	—	43	69	13	—	4	11	15	26	10	21	*	1	7	—
Institute of Lifetime Learning	—	32	76	10	—	1	7	23	20	11	40	—	—	10	—
Museum	30	40	90	10	10	40	—	—	20	10	50	10	—	28	44
Senior center or club	18	41	30	—	4	5	—	11	2	—	7	13	—	9	—
Public library	73	59	72	24	56	25	*	1	11	19	13	17	—	—	—
YM-YWHA or Jewish community center	15	30	5	7	6	2	—	50	2	2	2	19	—	7	3
YWCA	64	64	67	21	54	27	1	12	21	9	6	—	—	3	—
YMCA	48	47	69	10	35	20	1	—	7	9	6	5	—	2	—
4-H club	43	35	39	8	31	13	—	—	5	11	5	10	—	5	—
4-H club	82	43	21	4	62	36	—	—	8	11	3	2	*	*	—

*less than 1 percent

Source: Academy for Educational Development, 1976

94

TABLE 5
Percentage of Institutions Reporting Local or National Program Sponsorship of Some of Their Older Workers

Type of Institution	Percentage reporting some workers through RSVP	Percentage reporting some workers through local volunteer programs
Public school districts	30%	28%
Two-year colleges	24	23
Senior colleges and universities	5	4
Institutes of Lifetime Learning	30	40
Museums	17	11
Senior centers and clubs	43	32
Public libraries	17	23
Jewish community centers & YM-YWHAs	39	15
YWCAs	32	12
YMCAs	20	7
4-H clubs	16	17
ALL INSTITUTIONS	22%	19%

Source: Academy for Educational Development, 1976

APPENDIX C

A Sampling of Outstanding or Unique Educational Services Provided by Older Persons: Responses to the 1976 Survey

Note: *Where a person's specific age is omitted, the correct assumption is that he or she is at least 65 and very likely older.*

Helping with the "basics"

Seattle: Walter Huffine has tutored middle-school students in math four full days a week for five years. (In 1975 he received a national award as an outstanding school volunteer.)

Dallas: Ross Hoover, aged 88, tutors elementary school students in reading and math five days a week, from 8. a.m. to 3 p.m.

San Francisco: Lena Mendleson, a great-grandmother, uses baseball statistics to teach math. Ruth Thias works one-to-one with non-English-speaking students two days a week (she has to transfer twice to get to school by bus). Janet Nickelsburg, the author of nine books on science, teaches science in "impact" classes in three schools.

Downey, California: In the Downey Adult School "one teacher is still doing an excellent job in a literature class—she was 80 years old last month."

Richmond, Indiana: Working for the Morrison-Reeves Library are Miss Mildred White and Miss Frances Peacock, both of whom "listen to children read and help with mistakes."

Mainstream instruction

Marietta, Ohio: At Marietta College, Professor R. Lee Walp, recently retired after 40 years in the biology department, teaches a course in children's literature, long one of his avocations.

Ithaca, New York: Knight Biggerstaff, retired Cornell professor, gives a college-level course on modern China at the high school.

Annandale-on-Hudson, New York: At Bard College, Isaac Bashevis Singer taught short story writing "in inimitable fashion."

Brockport, New York: Miss Elsa Logan, aged 77, teaches Chinese. She is retired from the staff of Roberts Wesleyan College, in Rochester, where she taught French and Geman for about twenty years.

Asheville, North Carolina: Three retired executives provide management training at the Asheville-Buncombe Technical Institute. "Do an excellent job."

Mansfield, Massachusetts: Ralph Gordon, a Greek classicist, works every day with the high school English department. He is 84.

Working in public and school libraries

Portland, Oregon: For nine years, Mrs. Ida Nickolson, a retired fourth-grade teacher, has walked two to three miles four or five days a week to help the librarians in two schools.

San Francisco: Nancy Bray, aged 86, trains all new volunteers for the annual book sale at the San Francisco Public Library; sorts, prices and boxes all donations; works 10 a.m. to 6 p.m. for the four-day sale.

Fort Smith, Arkansas: "Mrs. Pearl McLaughlin, retired school librarian, has worked many hours for the past two years in organizing a centralized library in one of our elementary schools."

New York City: The head cataloger at the New York Society Library supervises general cataloging, catalogs rare books, and supervises the conservation and restoration program.

Bridgeport, Connecticut: Without the services provided by Miss Constance Ball and Mrs. Lyla Moore, a school library could not have stayed open.

Administration

Waynesburg, Pennsylvania: Joseph D. Hart, a retired officer of a savings-and-loan institution, contributes his expertise to keeping the Eva K. Bowlby Public Library on a sound financial program.

Bryan, Texas: H. W. Cook, a former high school principal, has helped the Bryan Independent School District convert from the old "hand schedule" technique to much simpler computerized scheduling.

New York City: Recently graduated with a B.A. from John Jay College of Criminal Justice, Miss Beatrice Jackson organized, developed, and administered the student-run Legal Services Department.

Lincoln, Illinois: Lincoln Christian College's vice president for financial development came to his post after a long successful business career.

Sewanee, Tennessee: Edward Watson, a retired attorney, serves as secretary of the Lease Committee and Land Commission for the University of the South.

Work with handicapped, retarded, and other "problem" students

Greenwich, Connecticut: In the Greenwich Public Schools, Dr. Payson Ayres tutors at a school for the "trainable retarded" (besides tutoring a Japanese student in English and serving "as resource to schools in areas of health, sex education").

Newberry, South Carolina: Mrs. Thomasina Mayers, a retired Newberry County Public Schools music teacher, makes a special effort to see that the "trainable mentally retarded students at Gallman Junior High School receive a well-rounded musical background."

Morton Grove, Illinois: The adult-services librarian at the Morton Grove Public Library, 71 years old, "is responsible for service to the nursing home and to our blind and physically handicapped patrons, as well as planning, arranging, and hostessing the many film and lecture programs we offer."

Washington, Pennsylvania: The Citizens Library's program for "illiterate and functionally illiterate adults," which enrolls 48, uses two older tutors.

Omaha, Nebraska: At the YMCA, "our senior citizen works daily—2-4 p.m.—with our mentally retarded children, supervising and coaching the children in recreational and aquatic skills."

Arts, crafts

Atlanta: Rufus F. Tucker, a music teacher retired from the Atlanta Public School System, now directs band ensembles, tutors individual students, conducts cultural tours, and serves as a consultant for the career education program.

Chicago: Sol Courecwitz works regularly three days a week for the Field Museum of Natural History. From 1968 through 1975 he gave 5,666 hours photographing anthropology artifacts for the catalog.

San Francisco: John Humphrey has worked for the San Francisco Museum of Modern Art since 1935, became Head Curator prior to his semi-retirement, and is now curator of photography. ("Semi-retirement to John means a full day.")

Spokane, Washington: Mrs. Pearl Cleek has taught children how to do eggshell mosaic. "She is in her 80s, arthritic, and in a wheelchair, but a help and inspiration to many students at Greenacres Elementary School."

Kapaa, Hawaii: Bacilio Guertes, aged 74, president of Kauai Senior Centers, is "extremely active, especially in instructing school children in ethnic (Filipino) crafts."

Brooklyn, New York: One member of the Breukelen Senior Center has served as teacher of arts and crafts which includes "oil painting, ceramics, needlework, sewing, knitting, and any other A & C requests."

A miscellany of educational elders

Portland, Oregon: Mr. Walter Dholer, aged 73, is a full-time volunteer at a school, where for four years he has arrived at 9 a.m. and left with the children at 3 p.m. five days a week. "He takes care of the entire lunch count (relieving teachers), tutors reading and math, supervises cafeteria and playground, does all the ditto and mimeograph work for the teachers, and serves as the principal's right-hand man."

Roswell, New Mexico: On the Roswell campus of Eastern New Mexico University, Dr. Smith serves as teacher, tutor, and advisor, and puts what he earns into a student loan fund. He is 92 years old. "A great teacher."

Plainfield, Vermont: Royce P. Hein, president emeritus of Goddard College, serves the college as "continuing inspiration, teacher, consultant, and trustee."

Jackson, Kentucky: At Lees College (a two-year institution), Mrs. Robert Reitz "did outstanding work as a teacher-tutor-library aide, in addition to which she organized and taught a class in weaving for community adults."

Asbury Park, New Jersey: "Kaye Capron, 78 years old. All summer helps teach five swim classes a day at the Shore Area YMCA. All winter helps with all pre-school and adult swim classes. Has been helping for over eight years, and we could not do without her."

Carmel-by-the-Sea, California: At the Carmel Foundation (a senior center), "an 80-year-old transplanted Briton teaches dress alteration, a retired Marine general teaches wood carving, a former dress designer teaches knitting to a group of 80-year-olds."

Bothell, Washington: A member of the Northshore Senior Center, Sidney B. Feiwell, "tutors several Spanish-speaking, Vietnamese, or Chinese-speaking exchange students or refugees, from junior high age to adults. He creates his own program and meets with them weekly at specified schools."

Portland, Oregon: In the Multnomah County 4-H Program, Mr. Earl DeWald "has served as Poultry Science Resource Leader, as 4-H Poultry Club Leader, as supervisor of numerous 4-H programs, and as a member of the county 4-H Executive Council (all in the last eight years. He's 83 years old!)"

APPENDIX D

A Selected List of Local Programs and Projects in Which Older Persons Are Educating Others

EDUCATING YOUTH

School Programs

DOVES (Dedicated Older Volunteers in Educational Services)
Los Angeles City Unified School District
Volunteer and Tutorial Programs
450 North Grand Avenue, Room G-114
Los Angeles, California 90012
    Joan Suter, Project Leader   (213) 625-6900
See pages 42-44 for program description.

Older Adult Project
New York City School Volunteer Program
20 West 40th Street
New York, New York 10016
    Ricki Rubinstein, Director   (212) 563-5620
See page 44 for program description.

Project M.O.V.E. (Miami's Older Volunteers in Education)
School Volunteer Program of Miami
Dade County Public Schools
2121 Ponce de Leon Boulevard
Coral Gables, Florida 33134
    Dr. Archie Jackson, Coordinator of
        Volunteer Services   (305) 442-8862
See page 44 for program description.

STEP (Senior Tutors for Educational Progress)
Redding School
Lonetown Road
Redding, Connecticut 06875
   Rosalie Saul, Project Director   (203) 938-2519
See page 45 for program description.

Takoma Park Elementary School RSVP Volunteers
Montgomery County Retired Senior Volunteer Program
14 Maryland Avenue
Rockville, Maryland 20850
   Godfrey Beckett, Director   (301) 279-1374

Since January 1973, fifteen RSVP volunteers have been spending a day each week with children in the Takoma Park Elementary School, assisting in one Head Start class and two kindergartens. They read aloud, listen to children read, and help them with simple art projects. Some help children practice their English in the English Speaking for Other Languages (ESOL) program. Others work in the art room, making word games and other teaching aids. Volunteers work from 9:30 to 11:30 a.m. and from 12:30 to 2:30 p.m. During lunch hours the RSVP and area school staff conduct a series of informal, in-service training sessions for the volunteers. Funding for the volunteers' lunches is an annual item in the Montgomery County School budget.

Teaching-Learning Communities (T-LC)
Ann Arbor Public Schools
600 West Jefferson
Ann Arbor, Michigan 48103
   Carol H. Tice, Project Director   (313) 994-2354
See pages 46-47 for program description.

Volunteer Talent Pool
Winnetka Public Schools
520 Glendale Avenue
Winnetka, Illinois 60093
   Mary Ann Manley, Director,
     Resource Center   (312) 446-9400
See pages 41-42 for program description.

Willoughby-Eastlake City School District
Office of Career Education
301 East 293 Street
Willowick, Ohio 44094
  Marge Lienert, Director   (216) 946-5000 x206

This program, funded jointly by RSVP and the Board of Education, began in 1973 as a means to encourage good work habits among high school students, to provide them with social models, and to give young people an understanding of the ingredients of successful work and life experiences. Some 250 older volunteers serve in numerous roles, among them tutors, teacher aides, and guides.

Outside the Schools

Expanded Horizons
Virginia Polytechnic Institute & State University
Extension Division
150 West Main
Abingdon, Virginia 24210
  Neel Rich, Project Director   (703) 628-6033
See pages 47-48 for program description.

Hand-in-Hand: Cross-Age Interactions
Girl Scouts of the U.S.A.
830 Third Avenue
New York, New York 10022
  Judy Cook, Director of Program
    Department, Educational Services   (212) 751-6900

Although local Girl Scout councils in communities across the country have for years run projects concerned with the elderly, Hand-in-Hand was the beginning of what Girl Scouts of the U.S.A. calls "the systematic development of a program design that would make it possible for every Girl Scout council to be involved with senior citizens in some meaningful activity." In the fall of 1974, with a two-year model project grant from the Administration on Aging, seven local Girl Scout councils (one each in Oregon, Wisconsin, and California, and four in Michigan) mounted special pilot projects to join Scouts and older people in entertainments, camping, and other events, with particular emphasis on reciprocal teaching/learning in arts and crafts. Girl Scouts learn from grandparents and great-grandparents how to plant gardens and can fresh produce. City girls go on overnight camping trips to farms and learn how to operate farm equipment from 65-year-old farmers. Seventy-year-olds, lead hiking and camping expeditions. Hand-in-Hand model projects, as developed and tested, are now available to all 359 Girl Scout councils (and their 3.2 million members) across the country.

Project Concern: Adopt a Grandparent
Cooperative Extension Service
University of Nebraska-Lincoln
4-H/Youth Development
114 Agriculture Hall, East Campus
Lincoln, Nebraska, 68583
   Elaine M. Skucius, Associate
      State Leader   (402) 472-2805

In 1976 this project was introduced in 4-H chapters throughout the state of Nebraska. The major goal of Project Concern is to establish a learning exchange between generations, whereby the talents of older people and the talents of youngsters can provide mutual benefits.

EDUCATING ADULTS

In Colleges and Universities

Folk Craft Project
Yavapai College
1100 Sheldon Street
Prescott, Arizona 86301
   Anna Kaspar, Coordinator of
      Folk Crafts   (602) 445-7300

During the 1976 fall semester, Yavapai College began a search for people 65 and over skilled in old folk crafts and willing to teach courses in these endangered arts to adult students of all ages. The outcome was the employment of fifteen instructors, ranging in age from 65 to 81, for 25-hour workshops in nine crafts: folk toys, old-fashioned rug making, quiltmaking, crazy patch quilt techniques, dried floral arts, tatting, spinning-wheel construction, primitive metal crafts, and apple dolls. Folk Crafts, now in its second year at Yavapai, operates on a very modest budget with in-kind assistance from the college. In 1977 the program was introduced at nearby Verde Valley College.

Hastings College
65 Club
University of California
San Francisco, California 94102
    Dr. Francis Seidler, Associate Dean   (415) 557-1320

See page 49 for program description.

Heritage Arts Program
Fort New Salem
Salem College
Salem, West Virginia 26426
    John Randolph, Director   (304) 782-5011

Salem College employs between ten and fifteen older artisans to teach authentic methods of quilting, chair caning, weaving, spinning, blacksmithing, basketweaving, and other folk skills as part of the arts curriculum. The program, housed in a reconstructed group of log buildings near the campus, has brought the college recognition in regional magazines and in a book published by the National Geographic Society.

La Verne College
1950 Third Street
La Verne, California 91750
    Armen Sarafian, President   (714) 593-3511

See pages 49-50 for program description.

Retired Volunteer Service Corps
University of Maryland
College Park, Maryland 20742
    Robert E. Shoenberg, Dean, Office of
        Undergraduate Studies   (301) 454-0100

Under the joint sponsorship of the Office of Undergraduate Studies and the Center of Aging of the Division of Human and Community Resources, this program began in the fall of 1977. Twenty volunteers were recruited in the Washington, D.C. area from among retired executives and professionals who have worked in business, industry, government, arts, human services, education, law, medicine, and the military. During the first year volunteers were assigned as Career Development and Internship Specialists. These roles combine work with students and on-going contact with professionals in the volunteer's career area. In the program's second and third years, roles will be expanded to include preprofessional advising, counseling students in academic difficulty, developing cultural workshops, and tutoring. It is expected that some volunteers will become adjunct instructors. Volunteers are asked to make a commitment of one semester (16 weeks) and in most cases serve for six hours a week. They have the option of continuing on for additional semesters, and of serving more hours per week if they wish.

Senior Consultants Program
Chabot College
25555 Hesperian Boulevard
Hayward, California 94545
    Gwen Yeo, Coordinator   (415) 782-3000 x476

Under this program, seniors provide volunteer service to the college, particularly in career and general education programs. Senior Consultants review and evaluate existing or proposed programs in job training, serve as guest lecturers or resource people in college classes, advise on a wide range of college activities, and participate in the college's tutoring program. A speaker's bureau made up of seniors makes special programs and speakers available on a wide variety of topics to senior groups.

Seton Hall University
South Orange, New Jersey 07079
    Emma G. Quartaro, Director of
        Social Work   (201) 762-9000 x401

Older adults, as special lecturers in a course on "Social Psychology of Aging," discuss how they have (or haven't) prepared for aging, retirement, and new patterns of living. The course is attended by students planning careers in social work with a special emphasis on the concerns and needs of the elderly.

University of Oregon
Center for Gerontology
1627 Agate Street
Eugene, Oregon 97403
  Frances Scott, Director,
    Center for Gerontology   (503) 686-4207

Older people participate as "teacher-learners" in the University's gerontology program. For eight years a seminar on the "Psychology of Aging" has been structured around teams comprised of a gerontology student and a retired consultant, who work together during the term sharing life experiences. In 1977 over 200 older adults had served as "retired consultants" and "teacher-learners" in this course.

In Other Settings

Chrysallis Center
Saginaw Valley State College
2250 Pierce Road
University Center, Michigan 48710
  Rose Collamer, Director   (517) 793-5930

Older adults serve as resource people in this support and self-help program for nontraditional students. Since 1974, 950 people have taken part in the program, 77 of them aged 55 and older, as resource persons in various Chrysallis workshops. Among the retired people on regular call are a composer-musician, a poet, two public relations experts, a personnel manager, an historian, a writer, and a member of the Service Corps of Retired Executives (SCORE).

Independent School District of Boise City
Department of Community Education
301 North 29th Street
Boise, Idaho 83706
  Thomas Richards, Director of
    Community Education   (208) 345-9911

Twenty percent of the volunteer instructors in the continuing education evening classes are older adults. They also serve as special resource speakers, expertise consultants, and in many other ways provide curriculum enrichment in all the programs of the Department of Community Education, the Boise Schools Volunteer Program, and the local RSVP program.

Senior Volunteers for Monroe Reformatory
Senior Services of Snohomish County (RSVP)
3402 112th S.W.
Everett, Washington 98204
    Barbara Nies, RSVP Director   (206) 355-1112

See page 51 for program description.

In Business and the Professions

Executive Volunteer Corps
415 Madison Avenue
New York, New York 10017
    Commissioner Sydney Kushin   (212) 593-8964

Through the Executive Volunteer Corps, part of the New York City Economic Development Administration, eighteen successful retired businessmen offer free counsel and advice to people who own or plan to start their own businesses. Since its founding in 1966, the Corps' retired counselors have served over 80,000 persons.

International Executive Service Corps (IESC)
622 Third Avenue
New York, New York 10017
    Frank Pace, Jr., President   (212) 490-6800

See pages 51-52 for program description.

Senior Medical Consultants
30 East 60th Street, Suite 301
New York, New York 10022
    Dr. Joseph Moldaver, Executive
      Director   (212) 838-6047

See pages 52-53 for program description.

Visiting Professor Emeritus Program
Association of American Medical Colleges
One Dupont Circle, N.W.
Washington, D.C. 20036
 Dr. Marjorie Wilson, Director   (202) 466-5193

This one-year-old program of the Association of American Medical Colleges (which represents 114 medical schools) matches retired doctors, all with distinguished careers in academic medicine, with medical schools that need (1) visiting professors, (2) replacements for senior staff members on sabbatical, or (3) temporary personnel while the school is searching for permanent staff.

Volunteers in Technical Assistance (VITA)
3706 Rhode Island Avenue
Mt. Rainier, Maryland 20822
 Thomas H. Fox, Executive Director   (301) 277-7000
See pages 53-55 for program description.

EDUCATING PEERS

Continuum Center
Oakland University
Rochester, Michigan 48063
 Betty White, Coordinator,
  Older Adult Project   (313) 377-3033
See page 58 for program description.

Country Gathering
Northeast Kentucky Area Development Council
P.O. Box U
Olive Hill, Kentucky 41164
 Regina Fannin, Project Director   (606) 286-4457

Country Gathering began as a federally funded nutrition demonstration project in 1968. It is now sponsored by the State of Kentucky and operates eleven centers in five counties in Appalachia. The program includes group dining and home-delivered meals as well as handicraft classes, nutrition education, and consumer education programs taught by volunteer retired teachers and staff assistants.

Duke Institute for Learning in Retirement
Office of Continuing Education
Duke University
107 Bivins Building
Durham, North Carolina 27708
   Jean O'Barr, Director   (919) 684-6259
See pages 72-73 for program description.

Elder Craftsman, Inc.
851 Lexington Avenue
New York, New York 10021
   Jane Robbins, Executive Director   (212) 861-5260

This program, initiated five years ago, operates under contract with the New York City Department for the Aging as part of the New York State Recreation for the Elderly program (administered by the New York State Office for the Aging, as well as with grants from the New York State Council on the Arts and from private foundations). Through the program older people affiliated with an organization (individuals not accepted) are taught craft skills that they in turn teach other oldsters at their centers, clubs, or nursing homes. The workshops are free, and most consist of 2-hour weekly lessons for a period of six weeks. Participants are taught ceramics, basketry, jewelry, leatherwork, and a variety of fabric and needle arts, among other crafts. The project has served over 300 different organizations in the New York City area.

Fromm Institute for Lifelong Learning
University of San Francisco
University Center Building, Room 538
2130 Fulton Street
San Francisco, California 94117
   Mildred Mishkin, Program Director   (415) 666-6320
See pages 55-56 for program description.

Harvard Institute for Learning in Retirement
Center for Continuing Education
Harvard University
B-3 Lehman Hall
Cambridge, Massachusetts 02138
    Jeremy W. Rusk, Assistant Director
       of Continuing Education   (617) 495-4973

See page 73 for program description.

Institute for Retired Professionals
New School for Social Research
66 West 12th Street
New York, New York 10011
    Hyman Hirsch, Director   (212) 741-5682

See page 55 for program description.

Institute of Study for Older Adults
New York City Community College
Division of Continuing Education
300 Jay Street
Brooklyn, New York 11201
    Peter Oppenheimer, Director   (212) 643-8150

See page 56 for program description.

Senior Actualization and Growth Explorations (SAGE)
Claremont Office Park
41 Tunnel Road
Berkeley, California 94705
    Eugenia Gerrard, President   (415) 841-9858

See pages 57-58 for program description.

PROVIDING SPECIAL EDUCATIONAL SERVICES

John Deere Tractor Company
400 Westfield Avenue
Waterloo, Iowa 50704
    Mary Ann Johnson, Director of
      Building Services   (319) 235-4871

Over 60 retired employees of John Deere have been hired as tour guides to escort an estimated 30,000 tourists per year through this Iowa plant. John Deere has found that their retired employees are natural guides; not only do they know about the plant and tractor building processes, they also care about the company's "image." The hiring, payroll and paperwork for this program are handled by Manpower, Inc., the national "temporaries" agency. Because the guides are actually employed by Manpower, who contracts their services to John Deere, retirement benefits are not affected.

Language Bank
The City Hospital Center at Elmhurst
79-01 Broadway
Elmhurst, New York 11373
    Emily Guttchen, Director of
      Volunteers   (212) 830-1271

See pages 61-62 for program description.

Legal Counsel for the Elderly
1424 Sixteenth Street, N.W., Suite 401
Washington, D.C. 20036
    Wayne Moore, Project Director   (202) 234-0970

See pages 60-61 for program description.

Senior Surrogate Parent Program
Institute on Aging
University of Miami
Coral Gables, Florida 33124
    Joseph Middlebrooks, Director   (305) 284-2490

See pages 59-60 for program description.

Tax-Aide Program
NRTA/AARP
1909 K Street, N.W.
Washington, D.C. 20049
  William C. McMorran, National
    Coordinator   (202) 872-4706

See page 61 for program description.